VO 101

Everything You Need to Know

To Start a Voiceover Career

Gabrielle Nistico

Author Gabrielle Nistico
Editors Karen Souer, Eric Schwabenlender
Additional Editing Eric Simendinger & Lewis Banks
Cover Design Brandon Falls

First printed 2005

Printed in the United States of America

Published by Three Moon Media

900 Mt. Holly Holly-Huntersville Rd.
Charlotte, NC 28214

GabrielleNistico.com
Voicehunter.com
VOPrep.com

Acknowledgments

The author would like to acknowledge the following individuals for their hard work, dedication, and support of this book. Adam Goodman, Eric Simendinger, Brandon Falls, Lewis Banks (LewisBanksVO.com), Anastasia Pinkham, Angela Oberer, Karen Souer, Alisha Fleming, Chris Thomas from VO Edit by Design, Angelique Coppernoll, the thousands of voiceover talent I have worked with over the years and *all* of my voiceover students.

"To over simplify a bit, there are two kinds of voice talent. Those who read the words on the page. And those who communicate the idea behind the words. I think we want the latter."

- This quote was part of the direction provided by a voiceover client casting for a non-union industrial project in the fall of 2014

Message from the Author

Dear Reader,

I write this while contemplating my own voiceover journey which includes triumphs, failures, wonderful mentors & learning many lessons 'the hard way'.

I set out to create a book for aspiring VO talent that is truthful & realistic about the business of being a voiceover performer. Thanks to my colleagues, staff, mentors & Goods Entertainment CEO, Adam Goodman, I was able to do just that.

We don't make outlandish promises of fame & fortune in this book, nor do we paint a false picture of glitz & glamour. Instead we have created a training guide for people who seek the truth, which is; that with hard work & dedication anything is possible, including a rewarding career in voiceovers.

Like me, & all the voiceover artists before & after me, you *will* find your success in this industry. It may not be the same as someone else's but it will be yours.

While I do not believe that there are 'secrets' to VO success, I do believe there are tactics & strategies that are well guarded. This book contains the information I found hard to obtain in my early years as a VO student.

I am in many ways still a humble student of this business. I learn something new every day & so will you. Thank you for your eagerness to learn & for teaching me. For with your feedback and guidance my voiceover journey continues to the next chapter.

Gabby Nistico

TABLE OF CONTENTS

Introduction

A career in voiceovers is a rewarding venture filled with creativity, art and entrepreneurial spirit. There is no limit to the success one can achieve in VO. Your ability to make money and have a rewarding career is relative to the time, money and effort you put into your business.

Building a business may seem daunting right now, but it's critical that you have an eye towards business if you want to pursue this path. Most voiceover talent own and operate a one-man shop. Their voice is their product and they are also their own sales force, accountant / money manager, marketing director, public relations person, receptionist and audio engineer.

Take some time to consider your current computer knowledge, your money management skills and your comfort level with sales. If you feel out of your depth in any of those areas then it may be wise to augment your VO goals with community classes and workshops that will help to enhance your overall business acumen. Likewise my other book, <u>How to Set-up & Maintain A BETTER Voiceover Business</u> will be of help.

As with any career you will need to allow yourself the time to learn the VO business while gaining necessary acting skill and voiceover experience. There typically isn't 'fast' money to be made in this industry. You will be a student for your first few years and a beginner or new talent for the 5 years or so to follow. This is typical.

We cannot stress enough the value of community in this industry. Making friends with other VO talent and becoming active in the voiceover community will be a huge benefit to you now and in the future. Voiceover talents typically foster wonderful relationships with one another and are always willing to lend a helping hand to fellow performers.

If you are juggling work, play, family and your new VO endeavor then immersing yourself into VO books, websites and local organizations will be even more important. If you don't take measures to feel like part of this business you may always feel like an outsider looking in. That glass can be very cold when your face is pressed against it.

There are many wonderful voiceover companies, many of whom we talk about in this book; that will help you on your journey. However, in your quest for camaraderie don't fall prey to companies that make large and exaggerated promises. If something sounds too good to be true, it probably is. Beware the voiceover scammers! There are many, many cookie cutter style voiceover schools and institutions that 'teach' and churn out large numbers of 'voiceover actors' – most of whom have no business entering the industry because they've been trained so poorly.

It takes hard work and time to be a working voiceover talent. Steer clear of any company that promises to make you a star quickly. You should never pay for any VO service, class, demo, or workshop until you know exactly what you will achieve from the process. You should also review and research any company you consider working with by speaking with a large cross section of talent who have worked with them in the past. Find out just how confident and successful these individuals are with auditioning, marketing and selling their voice and if they have a sound plan for their voiceover future.

There are many VO classes, training companies and coaches that do not create working voiceover actors at all. Instead they do a wonderful job creating perpetual students. You don't want this to be you either. It's very likely that you will seek out the assistance of a coach soon. Make sure that the coach you choose offers you full and complete insight into the various areas of the industry. Be wary of those that only offer snack size bites of information at a time and continually want you to pay for more and more training.

Having a great coach does not guarantee success either. You must guarantee your own success! Work hard, stay positive, always be ambitious and you will reach your goals.

It's also important to understand that voiceover is an umbrella term that encompasses many, many, small independent areas of voiceover that are referred to as niches.

Many beginners think they have to be good at *everything* and that their voice needs to "do" lots of things. That's not really true. Voiceover is a boutique industry in that most actors have a niche and are experts in one or two areas of the industry. It's better to be great at a few things than mediocre at a lot of things. A lot of what I teach is designed to help you get specific about what you do best.

Know yourself and know your voice. Be honest and realistic about your strengths and weaknesses. Check your ego at the door and know that if you think something is really easy (too easy), you're probably not very good at it and need a lot more work. This business can and should challenge you to improve your skills in many ways.

At the same time, stay super confident about your abilities and know that you do have strengths. Understanding what they are will come from validation you receive from coaches, voiceover peers, agents and of course paying clients.

Chapter 1 – VO Glossary

Before you can get started in Voiceovers you need to learn how to "talk the talk." The voiceover industry has its own lingo & language. Learning these terms is *very* important. Knowing & understanding them will allow you to better interact with those already in the industry.

These terms will give you the confidence necessary to conduct yourself properly as you continue to learn more about voiceovers & performance.

These terms are common everyday expressions used by those in advertising, marketing, audio production, & voiceovers. They are so common that lots of industry professionals assume that everyone knows them. We have of course found this is not the case.

Review these terms often. Quiz yourself on definitions. Also, never be afraid to ask someone what something means, as this business changes often & new expressions & terms develop over time.

:15 / :30 / :60: When a colon appears before a number (at the top of a **script**) it notes the length of a voiceover or total audio in seconds. **:60** means, 60 seconds. The times above are the most common, but times may be provided for a portion of a script or even one line.

A.B.C: An ABC read is frequently asked for by a client in a recording session when they would like a line or phrase within script isolated & read three times, in a row. They may say; "Give me an ABC on line 7 with various inflections."

A.D.R.: An acronym for audio dialogue replacement. It is a process by which the audio of an existing video is replaced. A.D.R. is commonly used in movies, animation, television shows & commercials. It is cheaper to replace all or part of the audio in a project than to re-shoot video. Replacements take place in a client's studio so that a voice actor can match the original video.

AD-LIB: When an actor is asked to speak without a script, or to add 'flair' & enhance a script either by deviating from it, making things up or adding noises such as laughter, a sigh or even a sneeze.

AGENT: An agent is one person or can be an entire company of people that represent you as a performer. An agent works to book you jobs, get you auditions & negotiates terms & payments on your behalf.

AUDITION: Talent are expected to audition for a VO job. Whoever is hiring will provide a small script sample that you are required to record. You are competing against other talent so that a client can decide whose voice is best for their project. Auditions are short & should never be the full size of a project; a paragraph or two is usually sufficient. Auditions can also be known as **specs**.

BOOKING: A booking is a term used to describe a paying job. Someone is booking you (penciling you in) for your time. A booking should not be confused with a **session**.

BROADCAST: Refers to audio that will be aired on radio or television for the purpose of promoting & selling another company's product or service. All **commercial** work is broadcast work.

BUMP: To bump a **session** means to move it to another time or date. However it also refers to an additional amount of time that you can schedule at a studio in conjunction with a **session**. You or a client can request a 2 hour session with a ½ hour bump. The bump is an additional block of time. It is understood that should that extra ½ hour not be needed you won't have to pay for it. However it ensures that if the extra time is needed it is reserved.

BUY-OUT: A buy-out means that the work you perform & the VO recorded will become the sole property of the person that hired you after you have been paid. You are waiving the right to **residuals** when you agree to a buy-out. Unless otherwise stated non-union VO jobs are typically buy-outs.

CALL BACK: A second **audition** to help the client decide between several very good **talent** that would work well for a project.

CAMPAIGN: An advertising campaign or a campaign of work is a series of similar type material for the same end **client** or user. You might be asked to record a 10 **spot** campaign for a car manufacturer, for example.

CASTING: Casting is the process by which a talent is selected for a project. The terms **booking** and casting are interchangeable. Casting can also refer to the casting industry which is made up of casting directors who have the job of finding and booking talent for work.

CASTING CALL: A casting call is an open call for **talent** to **audition** or submit a demo for work. The **client** probably has a particular sound or style they are looking for so follow the instructions / requirements of the casting call carefully.

CLIENT: A client can be one of two parties. Anyone who hires you for a VO is your client. They can be an advertising agency, a producer or a casting director. However there is also the END client. The end client is defined as the party or company the recording is actually for.

COMMERCIAL: A commercial is either a stand-alone advertisement or part of a **campaign** that includes a series of commercials. In relation to voiceovers the most commonly discussed commercials are those being used for radio & TV. A commercial is more commonly referred to as a **spot**.

COPY: Copy is the page or pages provided by a client that make up the project you are recording. Copy comes in many different formats & none ever really look alike. Copy is also known as a **script**.

DELIVERY: Delivery sometimes refers to how audio should be delivered to its destination but more commonly with voiceovers it refers to the "delivery style" a **talent** is being asked to use. There are many different ways to interpret **copy**; you always want to make sure you are providing an appropriate delivery. A common question to ask a **client** is: "Do you have any specific delivery instructions?" Meaning, how would you like the performance to sound. (Also see **direction**).

DEMO: The sample audio that talent use to obtain work. Talent may have one or numerous demos to showcase their abilities. Demos are traditionally comprised of work that you have been paid / hired to do previously & it's a composite or montage of your best performances. However, they are frequently engineered or created in-studio to ensure a controlled and marketable product.   It's the audio equivalent of a model's portfolio or picture book so great time and care are taken in their creation.

DIRECTION: In a way it is a road map but not in the sense of east or west. Direction is the way you are being directed to read the **copy** either by a **client** or **producer**. Often times it deals with an emotion or acting style such as: sad, happy, angry or "in a soft whisper." Talent will often ask – "What's my direction?" Or "Has the client asked for a specific direction?"

DISCLAIMER: Appears at either the very beginning or very end of a **commercial** & is typically read very quickly. It contains legal information that is required within the **spot**, usually in conjunction with a particular sale, contest rules or other participation restrictions. They are most easily identified when hearing an advertisement for a car dealership or contest rules such as 'No purchase necessary, void where prohibited'.

DONUT: Not the kind you eat, hence why it's spelled differently. A donut is a small piece of audio in the middle of a **commercial**. The **spot** will have a beginning, a blank hole & an end. The donut (hole) is used to give location specific information or sale information. It's a way to tailor a **spot** with additional info without having to change the entire **commercial**. You may be hired to record a **commercial** but not its "donut hole" or vice versa. It's also not uncommon for a voice artist to be hired to record one **commercial** with 15 different **donuts**.

DUB: To make a copy of a previous or master recording. Usually dubs are tangible copies that are distributed to multiple parties on CD.

INDUSTRIAL: Industrial work is **non-broadcast**. The term usually applies to video presentations & short films that are designed to teach a skill or task to its viewer. Industrial voiceovers are often times long recordings that are very technical in nature.

LEVEL: To **"give a level"** means that you are speaking into the microphone so that the **sound engineer** or **producer** can set the equipment to obtain the proper output recording level from the microphone; i.e. the volume. You will be asked to do so when they are ready. "Test, test, one-two, one-two" is the most common example – or you can just start reading a piece of the **copy** you are there to perform.

LOCAL: Local means that the audio being discussed will only air in the **market** being discussed. If you get a call from a client in Jackson, Mississippi & the commercial they need you to record is for "local use" then it will only be broadcast in Jackson. This term plays a key role in how much you will be paid for the **VO** you are providing, but usually only matters for **broadcast** voiceovers.

MARKET SIZE: Refers to the city in which your **VO** will be used. Market size often determines how you will be paid. A **VO** for use in New York City will cost more than for Evansville, Indiana. The larger the market size, the lower the number. Market #1 is NYC, Market #6 is Philadelphia, PA, Market #25 is Charlotte, NC, – the fewer people, the smaller the market size. The larger the market, the more money you make. Market sizes change as areas grow or decrease in size.

NATIONAL: Means that the audio being discussed will be broadcast nationally & heard all across the United States. This term plays a key role in how much you will be paid for the **VO** you are providing but usually only matters for **broadcast** voiceovers.

NON-BROADCAST: Refers to audio that will not be aired on radio or TV for the purpose of selling something. For the most part anything other than a **commercial**, **TV Promo** or TV Narration is non-broadcast.

PICK-UP: This is an abbreviation for "pick it back up" or "pick-up where you left off." When a talent flubs a line or makes a mistake on mic they find a natural pause point that occurred a few seconds earlier in the script & continue again from that point. They usually say, on-mic; "pick-up" before starting again. It becomes a verbal marker for the **producer** that a mistake must be deleted or corrected later on.

PRODUCER: This is the person who runs the recording session. You are behind the microphone & they are behind all the other equipment. This is the person who most likely will be finishing the audio **production** that you are providing a voiceover for. A producer is often times also called a **sound engineer**.

PRODUCTION: The production is the final piece of audio once your voice & all music & sound effects have been mixed & edited together to complete the final presentation. Production can also refer to an entire industry as in Audio Production.

RADIO IMAGING: Imaging refers to both a type of voiceover & a style of audio production. These are short pieces of audio that radio stations pay for. They air between songs & help listeners to identify the station & its overall message to the public. Styles of imaging are varied & complex. It is a branding & marketing tool that radio uses to gain & retain listeners.

REGION: Refers to a region in the country where audio will be used. Southeast, mid-west, etc. This term plays a key role in how much you will be paid for a VO but usually only matters for **broadcast** voiceovers.

RESIDUAL: Additional money you receive for work you previously recorded. In a pre-arranged agreement a voiceover can be "leased" for a block of time & a client can only use the material for that period (anywhere from 13 weeks to 1 year). After that, the client pays a residual if they want to continue to use the VO.

RETAINER: To be paid on retainer means that you have entered into a long-term, binding contract with a **client**. Both parties have agreed upon a specific quantity of work in exchange for a specific dollar amount. Both the work & payments are split up over time so that both parties are receiving (money or services) consistently throughout the contract.

SAG-AFTRA: The Screen Actors Guild / American Federation of Television & Radio Artists is the union that voiceover actors may join, especially those looking for a career in animation & move trailers.

SCALE: Scale is a rate of pay established by the union. It is a guideline & a base level of acceptable payment for a unionized talent, the minimum amount of money they can earn in a particular category.

SESSION: Refers to a recording session. It is an appointed block of time in which a **talent** will record for a paying client. To be "in a session" means you are currently recording. A session can be held in your studio, the client's or a third party's recording facility.

SFX: Short for sound effects. Usually found as an abbreviation on scripts & as a director's note on other documents related to a piece of audio **production**.

SLATE: Talent are asked to slate prior to beginning a recording session. Many talent even slate when recording an audition. It helps to identify the project & the talent reading. A typical slate would be "This is Suzy Smith reading for the Black & Decker radio commercial – part titled 'announcer'.

SOUND ENGINEER: He or she has nothing to do with engineering as we commonly think of it. This is the person who runs the recording session. You are behind the microphone, & they are behind all the other equipment. This is the person who most likely will be finishing the audio **production** that you are providing a voiceover for.

SPEC: A spec is a type of **audition**. If you are asked to perform on a spec basis it means that the company creating the final product is creating a sample or presentation at their own expense. The end **client** has not agreed to purchase the material yet. You are likely performing for free or small compensation, with an understanding that should the final production be to the clients liking; you, (along with everyone else on the project) will be paid upon the **client's** approval. If the material is never approved it will never be used & therefore is just an **audition** that never yielded a job. Know the size of the project as a spec **spot** is short. A spec **narration** might be large.

SPOT: A spot is either a stand-alone advertisement or part of a **campaign** that includes a series of spots for a client. In relation to voiceovers the most commonly discussed spots are those being used for radio & TV. Spots are also referred to as **commercials**.

TAG: A tag is a small piece of audio at the end of a **commercial**. It is usually used to give location-specific information or sale information. It's a way to tailor a spot with additional information without having to change the entire commercial. A tag always appears at the very end of a commercial & it's not uncommon for a voice artist to be hired to record one commercial with 15 different tags. It is similar to a **donut**.

TALENT: Talent can refer to a skill set or ability that a person possesses. But when it comes to VO, it means you! A talent is anyone that is paid to perform a voiceover.

TV PROMO: Similar to **radio imaging.** Promo VO airs during TV commercial breaks to promote other programs on the station as well as the nightly news. They are commercials that promote the viewing of more television.

VOICEOVER: Anytime a voice is recorded intentionally & with permission it is a voiceover. A voiceover can be used to sell a product, tell a story, or to teach a set of instructions. Often referred to in its abbreviated form as VO. Alternate spellings include: voice over.

The Voiceover Industry is loaded with its own language and lingo. Learn it and you'll feel like part of the club. Fail to learn it quickly and you'll feel like an under-graduate in a room full of PHDs.

Chapter 2 – Accent Loss & Improvement

Why does an Accent Matter?

Once a person decides to begin reviewing the necessary steps towards becoming a voiceover artists they quickly realize that they must become acutely aware of how they sound. You are probably in that position now. It likely didn't take you long to realize that if you want to speak for a living, you have to sound good. But what is a *good* voice? For starters, a good voice is traditionally defined as a neutral voice from a speaker that is devoid of an obvious accent or regionalism.

I often get asked a simple question: "Do I need to lose my accent in order to be in voiceovers?" The answer is not so easy. Is it a good idea, yes. "Is it absolutely necessary?" Well, that depends on your goals with regard to VO.

Typically speaking, it is expected that voiceover actors & performers speak better English that the average person. Therefore if you have an accent, it should be addressed along with any additional vocal concerns before you start to learn how to perform voiceovers.

An accent or regionalism could potentially alienate a particular population or group in the country and that means a loss of business or credibility for the company hiring you to perform a voiceover.

Alienation can occur very easily if conversational expectancy is not met. If you are appealing to a broad audience, like in the case of a national commercial & you have a discernable Southern accent, you will likely not be a credible performer to someone in the Northeast.

Accents come with a host of stereotypes & misconceptions. Whether they are false or not doesn't really matter. As voiceover people, we are not out to single-handedly change the views of the general population. We must instead understand things that can negatively affect our chances of booking work.

People in New York hear a southern accent & immediately make assumptions about the person who is speaking "Oh, they are slow, uneducated & *obviously* lacking culture". People in Charleston will hear a New Yorker & think; "That person is too aggressive! They sound so mean & rude!" We cannot change what the world thinks. What we *can* change is ourselves.

If you plan on marketing your voice skills & your talent to a region that shares the same accent as you, you might have a small measure of success in VO as your accent will be more accepted by the audience hearing your voice.

If you market your voice as an authentic accented speaker from a particular region in the U.S., you may find work as a character actor. This means that you are not being hired for standard everyday voice jobs but rather specialty jobs that require a unique voice.

But if you want to be taken seriously as a well rounded, nationally marketable VO talent capable of performing work for any client anywhere in the country then you must consider losing or significantly reducing your accent.

Very few of the professional voices we hear every day on the radio or TV have accents. TV and Film actors work very hard to eliminate their American accents in order to seek versatile roles. However, we are in a very unique time in the voiceover industry. Today's client is constantly seeking *real* voices. Meaning, voiceover actors that sound a little less poised and polished than in years past, especially in the commercial sector.

For the first time ever, we are seeing a demand for performers with subtle, mild or hints of accent and regionalisms. Clients are looking for voices that will stand out as being very genuine or real and nothing is more genuine than a guy from Philly or a gal from Fargo

– accent included. Collectively, the former cast of the Sopranos gets more voiceover and commercial work than any cast of any former TV show, ever. That's an amazing feat when you consider that nearly all of them have thick, authentic, NY / NJ accents that the actors play up or down at will.

The key to keeping your accent is marketing. Can you spin the potential negative into a positive? Can you alter or influence how someone might perceive your accent with the use of a proper branding? This topic will be covered in far more detail in later chapters. If you believe the answer is yes to most of those questions, you might be wise to keep the thing that makes you a unique speaker.

It would be wise to consult with a few voiceover coaches regarding your specific situation. The opinions you receive may vary but coaches will be able to tell you if there is money to be made with the accent you have.

You may also hear local performers such as nightly news anchors or disc jockeys that have accents familiar to the region they work in; but they are in a different industry. Broadcasting has different rules than voiceover. So don't let these differences confuse you or affect the way you look at your voice. You can't compare apples and oranges.

Assessing your accent, hearing your accent and manipulating or losing your accent are all attainable goals for a fledgling VO talent. And hey, you might not have an accent at all! It's time to find out.

Remember, in most situations, it's not what you say…it's how you say it.

"In order to change and improve your delivery, you first have to be aware of the way you speak. Most people mumble and stumble through life and don't know it. People have no idea how they come across because they don't hear their own voice the way others so. They're so used to it that they cannot be objective.

Our brains are conditioned to detect meaning, and to filter out fluff. I mean irrelevant sounds such as background noises, lipsmacks, breaths, and um's and ah's. Most of the time, we're not even listening, but we're interpreting what we believe the other person is saying, which is also based on their body language. Plus, every conversation takes places in a specific content which helps us determine meaning.

Now, take away the context, take away someone to talk to, and replace the conversation with a script. Bring the speaker into a small dark room, and have him or her talk into a microphone. Ask your wannabe to read the words on the page without making any mistakes, and make sure they know that critical ears will be evaluating every single sound. No pressure!

If you would, imagine yourself in that hot seat.

Unless you've had some traning and experience, you will quickly discover that the microphone works like a cruel magnifying glass. It exposes all the sounds you didn't even know you were making. As nerves take over, your mouth gets as dry as the Sahara desert.

Then you see the people on the other side of the thick studio glass, and you realize you can't hear a word of what they're saying. As you begin to read the first lines of the script, they start laughing, and you wonder: is it me they're laughing at? Am I making a fool of myself? What am I even doing here?

It gets worse.

When you're done reading, you're greeted with absolute silence. You can see the team on the other side, and it's clear that they're discussing something. They're not laughing anymore. If fact, you detect a couple of grim faces.

Finally, the sound engineer gets on the intercom, and says rather sternly: "Alright, let's do it again. Before you begin, let me play this first take back to you, so you can hear what we're hearing, okay?"

As you listen to yourself, you panic. This doesn't sound like you at all. Who is this person? What's up with all those loud breaths and shrill S-sounds? What did you do to produce that sickening symphony of mouth noises? Drink a gallon of milk? Eat super salty food? And what's up with all the mumbling? Before your internal dialogue sends you into a deep depression, the engineer has something to add:

"Let's try it again. This time, I want you to drink some water first, relax a little. There's so much tension in your voice. Please remember to E-nun-Ci-Ate, but don't overdo it. And one last thing, be you and you'll do just fine."

Whether on stage, in front of a camera, or in the recording studio, you're not hired to "just be you." You're hired to be your best, most professional self, and to make it sound (and look) perfectly spontaneous.

Voice actors are paid messengers. They're paid to get information across in a way that's easily understood and remembered. That's why your speech needs to be clean and clear. If it's not, it will distract from the message. In my experience, this is something the average person – regardless of their sound – is unable to deliver.

The average speaker is a lazy speaker. The professional speaker is aware and articulate. If you're thinking about becoming a professional speaker, you have to unlearn bad habits, and learn to dramatically improve your diction to the point where it becomes second nature. This is not something you can pick up through trial and error. You won't learn it by reading books. This needs guided practice, and lots of it. Compare it to learning how to play an instrument. It's not something you pick up overnight.

The goal is not to make you sound like an over articulated British stage actor from the forties and fifties. The goal is simply to be understood without having to work hard to get your words out. Once this becomes almost effortless you know you're on the right track. As that stage, you've become 'unconsciously competent.' You don't even realize that you're doing it."

- The Nethervoice, Paul Strikwerda @nethervoice
  From the blog entry The Worst Acting Advice Ever

Light travels faster than sound...this is why some people appear bright...until you hear them speak.

Learn how to change people's impression of you by improving the way you speak – it PAYS to do this, especially in voiceovers.

Dialects

Dialects are a fact of life. Every language has dialects that stem from different geographic locations throughout a country, a region, or even spanning different continents.

Let's look at the Spanish language for a moment. It is spoken in many different countries by many people around the world. If you think Spanish is Spanish is Spanish, you are mistaken. Speak to someone from Columbia, & they will tell you that the Spanish they speak is very different from the Spanish spoken in Mexico. The Spanish spoken in Mexico is very different from the Castilian Spanish spoken in Spain. And if we explore the country of Spain, we find that the same language is spoken differently in Madrid & Barcelona.

Likewise we will find that the French spoken in France is very different from French-Canadian and different still from the French in Haiti.

Do you think English is the same no matter where you go? People in England, Ireland, South Africa, Jamaica, & Australia all speak English. But the way it's spoken & the meaning of words can be very different.

In Britain if someone says; "Care for a fag?" They have just offered you a cigarette. In Ireland you might find "Bangers & Mash" on a menu. It's the daily special of sausage & mashed potatoes. These same concepts exist in the United States. Each area of our country has a different dialect. We'll explore them in detail a little later on.

Not everyone living in a particular region will share the same accent, but a good rule of thumb is that most will. There are many factors as to why a person may have an accent & why others might not. Let's explore some of reasons why a person might *lack* an accent that is typically associated with where they live. This way you can see if you likely fall into that category.

People who have moved around a lot & spent time in many different locations are usually the least likely to be affected by an accent, as is the case with military "brats". Their exposure to multiple & random locations usually results in a voice that is devoid of a connection with one particular area of the country.

Children who are the first generation of their family born in this country will often lack an accent. Or at the very least, those children will have a minimal accent compared to their peers.

This is because kids raised in a bilingual household or around adults with foreign accents usually learn a more neutral form of English. Brooklyn, New York has a very discernable accent. But a child raised in New York with parents from Israel is less likely to pick up a heavy New York accent.

As far as the rest of the country goes, there is a safe assumption that we can make; if the immediate area you grew up in (or spent most of your life in) is known for or associated with an accent, it is very likely that you have one.

If your parents have a well known American accent it's likely you have one. If you have traveled to other parts of the U.S. & have been quickly pegged as being from a certain area of the country, you have an accent.

It can sometimes be difficult to identify your own accent. Asking friends & family is usually of little value because if they share the same accent they won't detect yours.

If you are still uncertain as to whether you have one, ask someone from another part of the country. If you don't know a native from another area put a telemarketer to use! They call often enough; so make one of those calls good for something. Ask the sales rep. on the line where they are calling from. If they are in a very different area from you, ask them if you have an accent. Hopefully, you'll get an honest answer.

Accent Identification

Accents usually revolve around a learned speech pattern that entails the shortening, elongating, elimination or addition of vowel or consonant sounds. If you can identify the pattern of an accent you can learn to break its effect on your speech.

How do you overcome what you can't hear? Well, it's not an easy road, but it can be done. The first thing you have to do is take an honest look at yourself, the area you grew up in & the people around you currently.

There are a number of U.S. locations that are largely devoid of domestic accents such as Ohio, the Pacific North West, California, Utah, Nevada, Colorado, Iowa, & Kansas. These areas are known for their neutral American English. Likewise, there are a number of areas all over this country that dictate how we speak.

Take a look at the accents to follow. Look at where you live currently, where you've lived before & determine what the odds are that you have an accent. Go to YouTube.com to hear accent examples too.

NEW ENGLAND: MAINE - MASSACHUSETTS
An accent most noted for its exaggerated use of vowels and soft R.

Accent: I'm goin' tah paahck tha caah.
Proper English: I'm going to park the car.

There are varying degrees of this accent based on how close a person lives to Canada & how close a person is to Boston.

UPSTATE N.Y., CHICAGO, MICHIGAN
Similar to the New England accent, people that live close to Canada have a very notable speech characteristic - the long A. Resulting in a buzzy, nasal quality when they speak. The A takes on a whiny characteristic.

Accent: Sayhlee aahnd Aahndee kah-led
Proper English: Sally & Andy called.

NEW YORK, N.J., PHILADELPHIA

Probably the hardest of all U.S. accents on the human ear. It's known for many poor uses of the English language. The most common are the shortening of words & softening or elimination of all hard consonant sounds.

Accent: I'm gonna goes ova ta da grow-sree stow-ah an' pick up sum sow-duh.

Proper English: I'm going to go over to the grocery store & pick up some soda.

People with this accent also have a tendency to take mono-syllabic words & make them longer by adding extra letters. God becomes "Gauw-ud" or "Gah-duh". People who speak with this accent tend to drop their Rs too. Mother, father, & sister are said as: "muth-ah" "faw-thuh" & "sssis-tuh". People from these areas tend to talk "through their nose" resulting in a very nasal sound as well.

SOUTHERN ACCENT - VIRGINIA, THE CAROLINAS, GEORGIA, ALABAMA, TEXAS, MISSISSIPPI, THE FLORIDA PAN-HANDLE, LOUISIANA, ARKANSAS, TENNESSEE, KENTUCKY

This accent is the accent that best defines our country. Not only because more people have southern accents than any other accent but also because so many Westerns were the first movies exported overseas.

Accent: "Duh y'all wowna git sumthin tah eeet?"

Proper English: Do you want to get something to eat?

The further south you go, the thicker the accent becomes. If you go to Louisiana, Alabama or Mississippi (Miss-ippy), there's a much thicker accent. So thick in fact, other Southerners may have a hard time understanding the locals.

Accent: Y'all beaun don dair at duh feeshin pawnduh? Buh, day got sum big o' trot don dair.

Proper English: Have you been down to the fishing pond? Boy, they've got some big-old trout down there.

Southerners must also be careful of phrases & slangs that are only found in the south, such as "y'all".

One of the most common traits of a Southern accent is the exaggeration of vowel sounds. "I", "Y", & "O" sounds become very elongated.

SOUTHWEST: ARIZONA, NEW MEXICO, PARTS OF TEXAS & PARTS OF CALIFORNIA

People from these parts of the U.S. are heavily influenced by other cultures, like South Americans and Native Americans. As a result people from these areas tend to speak a bit slower than normal.

They almost sound as if English is a second language to them mainly because in many households & neighborhoods, English *is* a second language. The easiest way to describe this accent is that it sounds like a laid back, Americanized Spanish.

FARGO: THE DAKOTAS, MINNESOTA, NORTHERN MICHIGAN, PARTS OF ILLINOIS

A pleasant accent that is very mild. It is primarily heard in vowel sounds & it's the closest to a Canadian accent.

Accent: The keeds er ought an' abought tuh-night.

Proper English: The kids are out & about tonight.

This accent is best described as a cross between Canadian & Swedish. See the movie "Fargo" for a good frame of reference.

28 Days to Break an Accent or Speech Habit

Awareness is the key to losing an accent. Be extremely honest with yourself. Most new talent are absolutely shocked to the point of blushing when another industry professional tells them they have an accent. It can be a painful experience; don't let it blindside you. Know ahead of time what the odds are that you have one. Keep an open mind.

We explore the ways of accent loss much as someone would go about kicking a substance abuse or dependency problem. Clinically speaking, it takes 28 days to break a habit. From nail biting to overeating, it takes 28 days of dedication, patience, practice, & behavior modification to change a "bad" behavior. You need to think of an accent in the same way. If you have an accent, you are currently participating in bad speech behavior.

Fixing the problem lies in a three part process.

Awareness. You must be aware that you have a problem.

You must have the **Ability** fix it both physically & mentally.

Habit. You must replace old, bad habits with good ones.

Part one will be difficult. This book will help you to get on the road to awareness but you must become acutely aware of how you speak at all times. Every word, every syllable. The fastest way to achieve this is to record and listen to your voice with frequent regularity.

The process of accent loss cannot be limited to just your time on-mic or when working in the VO industry; it must be a constant & conscious activity in your day-to-day speech. We cannot effectively loose an accent if we do not make a *total* speech change. You may reduce your accent should you try to only make it an on-mic practice, but you will not eliminate it.

Making a total life change with regard to speech can be very trying. We typically don't think about how we speak; we just do it.

Compare your speech to the television. Mimic the way actors & actresses pronounce words. Ultimately, an accent is nothing more than a variation on the traditional or "correct" pronunciation of words. So, you must compare how you say things to the way others do.

Scrutinize the way your parents & siblings speak. If they mispronounce a word, you likely do too. Consult the dictionary for proper pronunciation & see if you really are saying something the way it was intended to be said.

Having the ability to change the way you speak is relatively inherent, just not easy. Most everyone has the ability to change their speech with lots of hard work & patience. Some people however, find that they are not just faced with the challenge of losing an accent. You might find that you have a speech impairment or other speech imperfection that is hindering your progress. If that is the case, your ability to fix the problem yourself is limited. You will need to consult with a speech pathologist or voiceover coach who can better assist with the problem.

Replacing the habit of pronouncing words the wrong way with the right way will need to be a constant & consistent effort. Training yourself to stop & repeat a word if you say it incorrectly is a very easy way to accomplish this. Just like when you were a kid. Likewise you should spend a few minutes, a few times per day practicing with lists of words you mispronounce.

The most challenging part of the process will be how unnatural correct speech will seem to you at first. Consciously pronouncing your words properly will make your speech sound very stilted & jerky in the beginning because the "new" words won't roll of your tongue easily. It will take time to become adept to the point where you can speak fluidly & seamlessly again. Practice is crucial & it will get easier with time.

More on Diction

Diction is the shaping of sounds, which joined together make words. Diction determines your understandability; and your understandability determines your acceptability. How easily and accurately you are understood has a lot to do with diction and articulation. It is also an indicator (perceived or otherwise) of your level of education. In voiceovers, it pays to learn how to speak better, literally. Diction can be divided into two parts:

1. **Articulation.**

   The proper execution of consonants.

2. **Enunciation.**

   The proper execution of vowels.

You must pay attention to the formation of sounds as well as lip, jaw and tongue movements that are needed to create the proper sound. Every mispronounced word falls into one of six errors:

1. Omitting a vowel
   - saying "GRO-SREE" instead of GRO-CER-Y.

2. Substitution of a vowel
   - Saying "GIT" instead of GET.

3. Adding a Vowel
   - saying "NAH" instead of NO.

4. Omitting a consonant
   – saying "GO-IN" stead of GOING.

5. Substitution of a consonant
   – saying "AXE" instead of ASK.

6. Adding a consonant
   – saying "IDEAR" instead of IDEA.

Most individual's diction errors will show a pattern. One or two diction errors will be common throughout a person's speech.

So, if you say "STREN-TH", leaving off the G in strength; you probably also say "LEN-TH", and leave off the G in length.

If you say "DIS" and replace the TH in THIS with a D; you probably also say "DAT" and substitute the TH in THAT.

Discover your patterns. Are your errors part of an area dialect? The result of lazy speech and not moving your mouth and jaw enough? Is there a particular letter of the alphabet that gives you trouble?

Practice will help you break those bad habits. Make yourself use problem words often and force yourself to correct the error by disciplining your speech during normal day to day activities.

Also, concentrate on making one correction at a time, for one type of error. Make the correct way a habit BEFORE tackling another problem area of your speech.

The mechanics of proper diction include exaggerated movement of lips, face, and tongue when forming certain sounds. Slowing down when you speak will also give you more control and the ability to think more about how you sound and the formation of your words.

Slangs & Other Non-Accents

The idea that kids speak another language is nothing new, especially to their parents. Since as far back as the '50's, each generation has created slang terms & phraseology all their own. Every decade, we see these language trends becoming more outrageous & more controversial. We also see these trends take us farther & farther away from the proper use of the English language.

Nationwide, we are being inundated by a speech epidemic that is most noticeable in people under the age of 30. Pop culture (be it in Hip-Hop music, generation X & Y movies or teen-television) is making the use of improper language…proper.

There is no place for this in the world of voiceovers. I doubt anyone reads the daily paper & "translates" proper phrases into slang terms. But what you may not realize is that making your speech more "colorful" by incorporating certain phrases and slangs may result in a sound that is unprofessional in a business environment.

The real damage happens on mic. If you have become very comfortable with speaking in slang, it might make you unknowingly sound uncomfortable when faced with speaking VERY proper English in front of a microphone. That will not only affect the way you read copy, but it will affect your performance, as well.

You want to begin training yourself to avoid slangs so that you don't sound as though you are struggling with the copy while performing. Starting to avoid improper uses of English will help you to sound more relaxed and natural on mic; otherwise, you may sound hyper-sensitive to pronunciation and the formation of your words.

Race can also play a role in American English. About two decades ago, "Ebonics" became an acceptable form of speech. While comedians often make jokes about Ebonics and it's affect on America, it is worth noting that most people can easily identify whether a person is Black or White based on how they speak over the telephone.

So, if you say "scured" instead of scared, "thang" instead of thing or "what-up?" instead of "what's up?" - you may want to consider revising your vocabulary. Ultimately, it comes across as an accent.

However African-Americans should not lose touch with their roots. A little known fact is that the voice community is in desperate need of more qualified, professional Black talent. The demand is very high. Often times when someone requests a Black talent they are looking for someone who genuinely *sounds* Black. Many African-American celebrities are being hired for tons of voice work too.

Remember how we talked about credibility & alienation earlier? Well, if you are trying to reach a Black audience, a White talent may not be the way to go. A spokesperson of a particular race will offer a more credible presentation to a group of the same race.

The African-American "accent" is typically called an "Urban" accent because it originated in large cities across the country & emerged as "jive" back in the '60s & '70s. Black talent should strive to be flexible enough to perform with or without an "Urban" accent. You may even strive to offer varying degrees of the accent for particular performances. A lot of people refer to Oprah Winfrey & Queen Latifah as having two voices - their TV voice & their "black" voice. African-American voice talent should work towards this type of vocal flexibility.

There are a handful of well known and highly respected Black voiceover talent whose careers you may want to explore. Rodney Saulsberry and Dave Fennoy are voice talent, voice coaches and Rodney has written many excellent voiceover books. Also notable are Jeffrey Holder, Bobbi Owens, and the owner of Voiceover Universe and voice of ESPN, Zurek. A web search will not only help you find these talent's demos but their websites and bios, as well.

Mistaken Identity: Other Speech Problems

Over the years, I have had many students come to me & say, "I have an accent". But upon closer inspection we come to find out that they in fact do not have one.

Often times, these folks are suffering from a mild speech impairment or vocal infraction. People, who mumble their words, speak with a clenched jaw or just have lazy speech often mistake their problem for an accent.

There is no easy way to identify your situation without the help of a professional but there are some things you can try at home if you think this might be you. The first is to really focus on pro-noun-cing your words. Remember learning phonics in school? It's time to go back to studying them. Phonics forces young readers to break their words apart & focus on each syllable. It might help you tremendously.

If you clench your jaw or talk through your teeth you want to spending no less than 3 minutes 3 times a day opening & closing your mouth as wide as possible. (Think BIG yawn). After a few weeks start to incorporate some copy into the exercise, reading with your mouth wide open. It will sound & feel funny but it will help you to speak more clearly over time.

If you mumble or 'chew' your words, stick a pencil in your mouth! Put a pen or pencil in your mouth horizontally & as far back into your jaw as is comfortable. Practice reading a few times a day with the pencil in your mouth. Yes, you will sound odd, but the pencil forces you to articulate & pronounce your words extra carefully so that you can be understood. Over time this behavior modifier will help you speak more clearly when the pencil is gone.

If you come to the conclusion that you have an accent then you must make a diligent effort to eliminate that accent before you can pursue a career in voiceovers. The loss of an accent can take years, but with persistence, you *will* lose it & it will be very worthwhile.

Essentially, you are going to re-train yourself to speak English properly, the way it was meant to be spoken. In some strange way you are learning to talk all over again. This time; you have the added benefit of already knowing what all the words mean.

Thousands of people accomplish this task every week. You can do it. And plenty more learn an even more amazing task – they keep their accent but somehow find a way to turn it off whenever they are on the mic. It's as if someone flicks a light switch & they start speaking in a totally different manner.

You can seek out the help of a professional diction & speech therapist or you can simply start taking voiceover lessons to improve the quality of your overall speech.

Some people choose not to lose their accent. They instead recognize it & use it as a marketing tool. They advertise themselves as a male or female with an "authentic" _____ accent. While might not receive a lot of work this way, it may be worth a shot if there is some other unique aspect of your voice that will set you apart. You may make a career strictly out of character work, in which case, you'd better start honing your character acting skills.

If you're still not sure if you have an accent we have included a list of the most commonly mispronounced words in the English language. Record the words on the next page & get a voiceover professional to evaluate the audio for you & see if you suffer from the effects of an accent. Or contact me. I'm happy to evaluate your speech & give you helpful hints based on your needs. 30 minute consultations are always free through my website, GabrielleNistico.com

VOCAL & PRONUNCIATION EXERCISE

Many people, even those without accents, sometimes mispronounce very common English words. This list below includes the most commonly mispronounced words and gives you a chance to practice them and see if you can detect any pronunciation issues that you may need to work on before entering a recording booth professionally.

MONSTER	FAMILY	HORRIBLE	DOT
AND	MOTOR	FOX	ASK
COFFEE	GOT	PEACE	METER
LOCK	MOTHER	DRAWER	BAR
FATHER	FLORIDA	DART	PEOPLE
HELLO	FAR	FOR	WITH
GUARD	PAPER	HARD	JAR
PALPABLE	GRAMMAR	DOG	ROOM
MARK	ANSWER	BETTER	COST
ORANGE	ABOUT	LOST	MOST
FIRST	HELP	STYLE	FIVE
NINE	DIAL	TABLE	SCHOOL
TWENTY	WOLF		

Chapter 3 - Performance

Now that you've begun the process of assessing your voice and any possible accent you may possess it's time to begin learning the true art of the voiceover industry.

The magic and the allure of voiceover really become apparent when you are able to express yourself and represent a client behind a microphone.

In order to make successful use of the information to come you will need a notebook dedicated to your voiceover performance studies. Some of the practice material in this book requires you to do some writing. Don't worry; you need not be a wordsmith.

It's also a great idea to use that notebook to write down questions. You will have many early on in your career and if you don't write then down, you're likely to forget them as soon as a reputable person whose brain you can pick becomes accessible.

You also need a microphone and a rudimentary studio. You can attempt to proceed without one but you may find it difficult to get the full benefit of the material that follows. You wouldn't try to learn to play guitar without having a guitar & you'll find the same is true here.

Any mic will do for now, even a cheap, 8 dollar USB computer mic. However, a mic like this is *only* to be used for practice, not for professional recording. You can also invest in a portable digital recorder or mp3 recorder. Neither will be practical for very long but for now they will give you a means by which to put the following information to use.

Having a steady supply of magazines & newspapers on various subjects is also a good idea. Virtually any text can be used to practice with so always look for scripts in common places.

What Is a Voiceover Exactly?

We're going to begin the journey of performance by taking a better look at what defines a voiceover.

Anytime a person's voice is recorded with permission & intent, it's a voiceover. Anytime someone reads a pre-meditated thought from paper & it is recorded, it's a voiceover. Anytime you hear a recorded voice that is being used to sell you something, explain something or interact with you in any way, it's a voiceover.

Voiceovers are not limited to commercials. There are many different types & styles of VO. Movie trailers, radio & TV imaging, cartoons, on-hold messages, in-store marketing, trade-show audio, promotional booths, pump side audio at a gas station, talking ATMs, the voice of self-checkout machines; even announcements heard in the grocery store are all forms of voiceover work & there are many more. Your phone's voice mail greeting (that you recorded) is technically a VO too.

By definition, the following are NOT voiceovers: disc-jockeys, TV anchors, on-camera actors, stage performers, live presenters, & public speakers. For the most part, if you can see a person's face while they are talking to you, it's not VO.

As an aspiring VO artist, you are about to take the steps necessary to become a master communicator that can effectively deliver a message to the masses. That ability is what makes VO a performance art. You are learning to be an actor, a storyteller, a salesman & a master vocalist all at once. It may sound like a lot of responsibility - and it is - but it's also incredibly fun and very fulfilling work.

The most common misconception about voiceovers is that all it takes to be successful is to have a great voice. Not true. Voiceovers are not about having the most beautiful voice. Think about how many grating, annoying, or even odd voices you have heard in national commercials, movies and cartoons. If the job is national or of large acclaim, you can be sure those were paid performers and for as unpleasant as they may have been, all those talent have one very important thing in common; they all know how to use the voice they have. You must do the same thing. Have you ever met someone who was not classically handsome or pretty but yet many people still found that person attractive? Talent who don't have a classically "attractive" sound still have a certain appeal that makes then listenable. And the most amazing models, who take gorgeous pictures, are usually a bit odd looking in person.

Another great misconception is the belief that in order to be a voiceover actor I have to perform everything and be extremely versatile vocally. Right now, you may think that your voice needs to be about to "do" lots of things.

That's not true. Today, VO is a boutique industry with actors who offer niche services. These actors are experts in 1 or 2 areas of voiceover. They are masters or a particular genre as opposed to mediocre at a lot of things. As voiceover actors we have some variety but not loads of it.

Those of us already in the voiceover industry talk to many people much like you, who all say the same thing: "I've been told I have a great voice all my life." =Your artistic performance determines whether you will be a great talent or just an "ok" talent.

When radio first became a form of entertainment, it was not because of music. The music came later. It was because of voice actors who performed audio plays. It was truly "theater of the mind" because listeners "saw" the story unfold in their head.

The first soap operas & situation comedies where introduced on the radio as audio plays. Many people "saw" Clark Kent turn into Superman for the first time on the radio. No, these old-time radio shows aren't voiceovers, but they are the predecessor to the voice industry as we know it today. They changed the face of storytelling forever & redefined how we looked at the instrument that is the human voice.

To indulge in a very worthwhile history lesson you can find digitally re-mastered CD copies of classic radio dramas in bookstores & novelty shops. Or take a few hours on a Saturday afternoon to listen to the last surviving show of its kind — "A Prairie Home Companion", hosted by Garrison Keillor. It airs on most public radio stations across the country. Not only will you be surprisingly entertained, but you will likely gain a deeper appreciation for the art of voice acting.

As an aspiring VO artist, you are about to take the steps necessary to become a master communicator that can effectively deliver a message to the masses. That ability is what makes VO a performance art. You are learning to be an actor, a storyteller, a salesman & a master vocalist all at once. It may sound like a lot of responsibility - and it is - but it's also incredibly fun and very fulfilling work.

Everyone Tells Me I Have A Great Voice

You too? Thousands of people try to enter this profession every year because someone told them they have a great voice. Unless the someone in question is a working professional voiceover actor, or a voiceover agent, it's unlikely their compliment holds any merit. You may very well have a very nice speaking voice; however this is not enough to determine if you will be a natural at voiceovers.

There's only one way to assess your raw skill in this industry and it's with a coach. Even a one-time on-mic session should be enough to help you determine how much talent you have. A good coach, will also be able to help you see the areas in which you need work and they should help you construct a plan. You'll use this data to determine your site reading, acting, vocal and technical skills.

Voiceover is so much more than just speaking. I'm going to pose a question that I'd like you to consider now, and as your journey evolves: are you a pretty voice or an ugly voice? A pretty voice belongs to a classic, polished speaker, someone devoid of an accent and who has excellent diction, enunciation and pronunciation skills. Pretty voices are very precise with excellent pitch, tone & volume control too. They thrive when a client asks for a voice that is proper & easy to listen to for hours. They are pleasant & friendly. Pretty voices make a living in corporate narration, industrial voiceovers, e-learning, commercials, long form projects and audio books.

An ugly voice does not take a backseat to pretty voice. Ugly voices are real, genuine, and flawed in a very human way. They aren't perfect – they have quirks, accents, and less control but this often makes them interesting to listen to. Ugly voice is emotional and raw and lacks the self-consciousness that makes us afraid of embarrassment. Ugly voice takes risks and thrives in commercial and narration work that requires a true storyteller.

Advertising & Voiceovers

Today, the most common voiceover applications are the ones used to support the advertising community. VO plays an important role in marketing, branding, & the process of buying & selling goods & services.

Smart advertisers know that consumers are not buying for the sake of acquisition. People make purchases for personal and emotional reasons. Their individual motives usually lead to a feeling of satisfaction and fulfillment after a purchase.

Think it's not true? Then why don't we all drive the same car? Wear the same clothes & buy the same toilet paper? More importantly; why did you buy that fancy new watch, jacket, handbag etc., that you just HAD to have?

Smart advertising focuses not on the product or service, but the meaning & change it will bring into the lives of the consumer. A great story dramatizes the *benefits* that dictate our buying habits. Since each buyer is unique, that's why there are so many ads (thousands are created daily). It's why the market can support such a wide variety of on-camera and voiceover actors. Each voice has the potential to speak to a specific buying group. That's why clients will spend a lot of time finding and seeking out the perfect voice for their ad.

More than 60% of all voiceovers are used & created for advertising purposes. The job of making a product appealing & motivating a potential customer to enter a store, call a phone number or visit a website is in the hands of the VO talent. It's a lot of responsibility and it's one of the reasons why it's so important that you understand how to use your voice.

There are a few common and frequently used formulas that advertisers rely on to reach a buying audience. Some are tricks, some are truths and some are sneaky psychology.

A large part of your job in voiceovers is going to require that you understand consumer groups & people's buying habits too. Call them techniques if you like; here's a few that work really well.

1) Allow the Audience to be a Voyeur.

   People love gossip. They love being privy to something that is secretive and that they really aren't supposed to know. By giving the audience a peak at something they aren't supposed to see, they are immediately drawn to the information being presented because they are intrigued and captivated.

2) Give a genuine Referral.

   Ask any salesperson what they want more of and they'll tell you referrals. Why? Because referrals work. More business is conducted and more transactions solidified whenever a person receives a referral from someone they trust. Be that trusted source.

3) Identify A Problem & Offer a Solution.

   When we have overcome a problem, obstacle or challenge in life, we are filled with a certain gratification at having 'conquered' an oppressive force. Therefore we want to share the solution with others and aid in their quest to slay the same beast.

Advertisers know that consumers aren't buying for the sake of acquisition. People make purchases for personal and emotional reasons. This leads to a feeling of satisfaction and fulfillment after a purchase.

LESSON #1: TALKING ALOUD

This lesson is about learning to be comfortable with how you sound in all situations. It requires that you talk! Yes, even to yourself.

Take time everyday to read out loud. Everything from newspaper headlines to street signs, even pamphlets in the waiting room at the doctor's office.

Reading to your children is a rewarding experience & also a great way to practice. Don't have kids? Read to your significant other - everything from romance novels to the stock report. At some point you need to practice with a willing audience anyway.

Reading & talking at the same time is one thing, but reading & talking with emotions is all-together more challenging. Reading out loud needs to be second nature to you so that you can focus less on the words on the page & more on the performance you are giving.

You'll become more comfortable with you sound of your voice and the nuances of your speech too. Probably the biggest benefit to this practice is that you'll learn to be fearless in the face of a mistake. Voiceover actors make mistakes all the time. We flub lines and words, get tongue tied and for the life of us, occasional, just can't get some words to flow fluidly from our lips.

You can't be daunted or flustered by your mistakes. They can and will happen. You must be as comfortable and confident with errors as you are with a great performance. So, the more you read aloud, the more mistakes you'll make. The more you make, the less embarrassed you'll be by them.

Goal: To be comfortable with hearing yourself speak while learning to sound less like you are reading from a piece of paper & more like you are telling a story.

Breathing

The act of breathing plays a very important role in a voice person's career. And don't snicker because it's not as easy as "in" & "out". The simple fact is, you don't breathe & talk at the same time. While you speak, you are either expelling or holding your breath & you don't take air in again until you stop talking. Proper breathing techniques ease your efforts in delivering copy. It also makes for a better read because you will pause less often to breathe and are less likely to run out of breath.

Professional studio microphones are very sensitive. They pick up noises that we make unconsciously. In the early stage of your voice career, it is your job to become conscious of every noise you make via your mouth & nose, & this includes breathing.

Voiceover talent typically breathe through their mouth instead of their nose when reading copy. The reason? You get only a normal amount of air when breathing through your nose. When you breathe through your mouth, you get much more air per breath. When you are exhausted from a good workout you, automatically start breathing out of your mouth because your body needs more oxygen.

Nerves also play a big part in breathing. When a person becomes nervous, it becomes harder to breathe. If you know how to control your breathing, you will stay calm under pressure while still being able to give a great performance. Concentrating on your breathing allows you to have more control of your voice.

Learn your voice's normal pitch. When it goes up because you're nervous, rely on deep breaths to calm you & get it back to normal. Remember that in VO, there is a fine line between the disaster of being self-conscious & the advantages of being conscious of self.

Singers often times make for excellent VO people mostly because they have been taught to breathe from the throat or mouth. They understand the difference between a "head-tone" & a "chest-tone" too. You may have heard the phrase "from the diaphragm" which means to speak & breathe from the lower recesses of your lungs.

Speak in what you consider to be a wimpy voice. You'll strain your throat a bit & will probably speak in a softer tone than normal. That's because you are using a head tone which may even make you sound a little nasal.

Now, speak in a big, deep booming, voice, like Barry White. You'll have to take a deep breath before you even start. You'll sound a bit unnatural of course but to get enough power to pull off such a big voice requires that you put a lot of air into your lungs. That is what it means to breathe from the diaphragm. Of course these examples are extremes. The next lesson will help you put your breathing into practical use.

Learning to isolate your breathing is also very important because it will make the job of the audio producers who work with you easier. Thanks to digital editing it is now possible to remove something as tiny as a breath from an audio session. It is common practice to edit & remove breaths, but the only way this can be done flawlessly is if the talent has isolated their breathing by inhaling & exhaling from their mouth only.

Talent must learn very early whether or not they make excessive amounts of noise while breathing. You must begin to self analyze your breathing. For instance, you may find that you should never exhale through your nose because when doing so you make a whistling sound. Everyone is different. You'll need to find a "silent" breathing method you are comfortable with.

There are voice trainers, mostly employed by singers, who can teach you valuable lessons in speech & vocal strengthening while helping you learn to master diaphragm breathing. It is an investment worth thinking about if your voice is truly to be your career & life.

Taking a Deep Breath

Stand up.

Take a deep breath.

What just physically happened?

When you tell most people to take a deep breath, physically they throw their shoulders back and chest out. Is that what you did? Unfortunately, those actions do not equal a deep breath.

Lay on your back on the floor. Place your hand, palm gown on your tummy. Take a deep breath!

What just physically happened?

This is proper breathing. When you lay flat on your back and breath, your diaphragm fills with air. You must picture your diaphragm as an inner tube that circles your mid-section. When you take a deep breath, the inner tube fills with air.

Stand up straight.

Place your hand palm down on your tummy, take a deep breath and push your tummy out.

You should feel the air fill in your back above your kidneys.

Breathing in this way will expand your breathe capacity and increase your air intake – this improves the volume and control of your voice. And helps to quell nerves. More air equal more voice!

LESSON #2: BREATHING POINTS IN COPY

1.

Choose a piece of text from a book, magazine or newspaper. Make sure it is something you can mark with a pen or a photocopy of the original. Stand; don't sit, in front of your microphone.

2.

Take a very deep breath through your mouth & read at a normal & comfortable pace until you run out of air or until your voice cracks or becomes shrill.

3.

Mark the spot where you stopped to breathe in red.

4.

Then in a different color mark a natural pause point such as a comma or period, about a sentence *before* where you ran out of air.

5.

Begin reading again from the beginning, only this time when you get to the earlier marking, stop, open your mouth, & take a deep breath. Hold that breath, pause briefly & then begin again from step 2 until the entire page is marked with the spots where you ran out of air (red) and the points where you *must* stop to avoid that problem.

Another variation on this exercise is to simple stop, breath, and pause briefly at each and every punctuation mark – whether you need to take a breath or not. Doing so ensure that you never run out of air and that you slow your pace and take your time with the copy.

Some voiceover coaches and methods recommend that you ignore punctuation altogether in a script. I don't find this to be wise or practical for some very important reasons.

When a copywriter creates a script, they are trying to give you cues and clues as to what it is they are expecting in your performance. Writers will often use punctuation to send you a message regarding how and where to pause within a script. Punctuation may be their only means by which to communicate with the voiceover actor as they may not have an opportunity to speak with you directly about the copy.

Professional commercial copywriters also understand that they are creating text that is meant to be spoken, not read. Therefore they may make grammatical choices that aren't literarily proper but that do in fact work well in spoken word. We don't necessarily read / write the way we speak. So, I recommend that you use the following formula to "play" your punctuation and use it to create a better performance.

(.) periods, (,) commas, (;) semi-colons = 1 beat of pause.

(:) colons, (!) exclamation points, (-) dashes, (/) slashes = 2 beats.

(?) question marks, (…) ellipsis', = 3 beats of pause.

Each pause is enough time for you to tap your toes, clap your hands or snap your fingers. You can use these pauses to plan and map your breathing.

Goal: Keep practicing until you feel that you have learned to anticipate, ahead of time, where you will need to breathe before running out of air. Remember to pause slightly before & after the breath. This is essential as it allows the breath to be isolated & removed in post production, which results in a cleaner & nicer sounding piece of audio.

How to Take Care of Your Voice

It should come as absolutely no surprise that your throat & vocal cords come together as the instrument of your career. It's only fitting that we take time to talk about the overall health & well being of this part of your body.

Like most parts of your body, your throat and mouth are made up of a series of muscles. Your tongue is actually the strongest muscle in your body.

Think about the muscles in your neck & back. When you go outside into cold weather, they shrink & tighten. The same goes for your throat, vocal chords & tongue. As a result, it's best that you drink room temperature or hot beverages especially before & during a recording session. Cold beverages (especially those with ice) will change the pitch of your vocal chords by causing them to tighten & constrict.

Dairy is often times cut out of many a voice person's diet. Many singers do the same. Yogurt, milk, cheese, & other items that contain dairy take away the purity of your voice & make it sound "murky" or worse yet, phlegmy. It's best to avoid these foods on the day of a recording session.

Alcohol, whether it be liquor or otherwise, is also bad for your throat. It's very drying & irritating to the throat. Caffeine in excess can dry you out too.

You want to avoid clearing your throat in the often times wrenching manner most people do. It's very bad for your vocal chords. Instead, try to cough. It's a more effective way of clearing your throat & it's less damaging.

Here's a list of great, all natural supplements for your throat. They are also very good to be taken for a sore throat or cold & best yet, they have no warning labels. All of these give your voice a clear, clean sound & while some of them may be a little hard going down, they are all very effective.

Note that we are not doctors – we're just giving you a list of easy to find items that many talent use & love. As always, it's best to consult with a doctor before beginning any regimen.

We also recommend that you seek out an Ear, Nose, & Throat specialist. A regular check up will ensure that your pipes are in working order & of course they can answer any questions or concerns you may have.

Honey – naturally coats the throat & soothes it.

Olive oil – naturally coats the throat & soothes it.

Lemon – nature's detergent – cleans out your throat & nasal passages.

Slippery elm root – is available in lozenges & throat sprays that work to help you get your voice back when sick – it's very soothing.

Mint tea (tea in general) – all around just great stuff!

Ginger – with its spicy kick, it helps to clear blocked airways, drain sinuses & makes breathing easier. Soft, chewy, individually wrapped ginger candies can be found in many stores and are a perfect way to make the effects of this spice very portable.

Pectin – found in some lozenges, relaxes your throat muscles, opens sinuses, clears congestion & works great to temporarily eliminate any tenderness from a cold or excess use of the throat. Pectin can temporarily help you gain back your voice when sick.

Hot or Luke-warm water & beverages relax the throat, soothe sore muscles & loosen the vocal chords. But…stay away from anything with a lot of sugar or lots of cream or milk.

Eucalyptus – Gets rid of stuffiness & helps you breathe better; it's the main ingredient in vapor rubs.

Pure Peppermint Oil – Not to be ingested! It helps you to breathe when stuffed up. Place some on a cotton ball & inhale the vapors or rub a small amount on your temples.

Entertainer's Secret – A throat spray that many singers and voiceover talent swear by. It is formulated to resemble natural mucosal secretions and designed to moisturize, humidify and lubricate the throat - available online.

Throat Coat – A tea and lozenge line manufactured by Traditional Medicinals. They help to soothe the throat when feeling under the weather.

Salt Water - to gargle & clear your nasal passage. A Neti-Pot is a great way to get all the benefits of salt water.

Hot Sauce - any kind will do. It makes all your senses come to life. Actors walk around movie sets with hot sauce in little holsters. It gives you a boost & brightens the voice.

If you have a day when your voice just isn't right or you're feeling under the weather but you still need to perform: brew some mint tea, add a pinch of ground ginger & a tablespoon of honey. Or, mix the juice from a lemon, a pinch of salt & a few drops of hot sauce. A similar concoction is a very spicy Virgin Bloody Mary.

Find what works for you – there are a number of home remedies and throat care regimes Some folks even swear by sinus rinses and Netti Pots. Experiment and determine what feels right for your body and your voice.

Note to Smokers

We all know it's bad for you. You've probably heard every warning imaginable and you know the risks associated with smoking therefore we aren't going to preach. However there are a few solid facts that pertain to your voice when it comes to smoking.

The average human voice changes once a year. These changes are subtle but become noticeable over time. VO people are more aware of these changes than anyone because they have documented proof of the changes to their voices in the form of demos & session work.

Depending on how much you smoke, your voice may change as often as every 6 months. So be careful. Today you sound great & the next thing you know, you have a smoker's rasp, & the damage done is irreparable.

Many older male voiceover talent have actually admitted to using cigarettes as a way to deepen the sound of their voice and make it richer; which does work for a short period of time. But the health risks simple aren't worth whatever small amount of added depth the cigarettes can impart to your voice.

Since men naturally have deeper voices than women, male smoker's voices are usually less affected, but the effects of smoking can be devastating to a woman's voice. The result is a very unfeminine, unsexy sound that NEVER gets VO work. The audio doesn't lie. If the effects of smoking are starting to be heard in your voice, please consider quitting if you intend to continue this career path. We know too many people whose voiceover careers and lives where ended because of cigarettes.

LESSON #3: WARM UP

Before a session, try to either sing or speak single syllables or notes with a natural delivery for as long as you can. Doing this 5-10 times will increase the strength of your chest, open your air ways, make your vocal chords more limber, get rid of "morning voice" & offer more speech between breaths.

Do you remember learning music scales in school? Who can forget this classic warm-up?

DO-RE-MI-FA-SO-LA-TI-DO

Try getting into the habit of using it again to warm up your throat, lungs, & abdomen, or try the following exercise.

This song works spoken or sung but is most effective when repeated with increasing speed. It's a camp song & you can find it on the internet with a little bit of searching.

SARAH SPONDA / SARAH SPONDA / SARAH SPONDA / RES-AH-SET

SARAH SPONDA / SARAH SPONDA / SARAH SPONDA / RES-AH-SET

AH-DOOR-EH-OH

AH-DOOR-EH-BOOM-DAY-OH

AH-DOOR-EH-BOOM-DAY / RES-A-SET

AH-SAY-PAH-SAY-OH

Goal: To feel the effects of a vocal warm-up.

Social Interactions and Your Voice

As a whole we all have a habit of "acting" differently with different people because it's just what is socially accepted or proper. In other cases, it's because we tend to be a bit guarded with our true feelings.

For the most part, we act a certain way, dress a certain way and speak a certain way because we know what sort of behavior, language & level of respect is expected from another person. Simply put, we change how we act in accordance with who we are speaking with in order to meet social expectations.

Even though people are all individuals; society (especially when it comes to politics & advertising) lumps human beings into categories called "demographics". The people who write voiceover copy work hard to define *who* the target audience is. They do this based on the information they get from the advertiser or client.

You must know & understand the demographic you are trying to reach. It is the key to all successful advertising. Otherwise, how can you effectively deliver a message, sell a product, or affect someone on an emotional level if you don't know who they are & why you are speaking to them?

Advertising dollars are only effective & well spent if a company succeeds in reaching their intended audience. Every buying group is different but there are similarities that help to determine a demographic. Demographics are based on age, sex, race, marital status, income, level of education, & the area in which a person lives.

Once those key points have been defined about a consumer group, a company can go about defining their primary advertising target or "core demo" by getting even more specific & evaluating everything from hobbies to leisure activities. Your spending habits, the car you drive, and the music you listen to… almost everything in your life is taken into consideration when advertisers are vying for you to spend your money on their products or services.

Ever fill out a product survey? They ask a ton of questions. Like, "How much do you spend on housing per month? Do you rent or own?" "How much money did you spend on groceries last month?" A survey like that is used to define the lives of a company's customers. That information is then assessed & used to better understand the buying habits & lives of the people that frequent a particular retailer.

Studying demographics and understanding them is not difficult. Whenever you shop, take a moment to observe your fellow shoppers. A shopping mall is a great place to study buying habits. Observe what types of customer shops at which stores. You will be able to make quick and simple generalizations that will help you to connect a product or store with a potential shopper. Restaurants are great places for this process too.

Pay attention to the buying habits of your friends and family, too. Everyone has a brand or product they are extremely loyal to. Ask them about their connection to these products and why they are so committed to their deodorant, shampoo, toothpaste, etc.

The answers you receive might surprise you. Familiarity and tradition are typically the number one reason for purchases. Chances are you buy many of the same products your parents did simply because you grew up with them. This, too, is something that heritage brands like Campbell's Soup, Skippy Peanut Butter, Clorox and Coca Cola capitalize on. In the next few pages we have provided a number of common demographics and we've connected them to specific products so that you have examples that will help you make these connections on your own in the future.

Examples of Demographics

Females between the ages of 12 & 24 who spend an average of $30 a month on beauty products, listen to pop music, enjoy shopping at the local mall, & watch teen based soap-operas on TV are the primary target for a company like Covergirl, that makes make-up, facial cleaners & other beauty aids. Their slogan is "Easy, Breezy, Beautiful…Covergirl." They employ popular, glamorous, female celebrities as spokes-models.

Men between the ages of 35 & 54, who earn $60,000 per year, consider themselves to be rugged & "uncomplicated" are courted by domestic truck manufacturer Chevrolet. Chevy has a full line of versatile, rugged, on & off road vehicles that can get him to work & to & from his next outdoor adventure. Chevy trucks are associated with the slogan "Like a rock," in conjunction with a popular Bob Seger song by the same name.

Married couples between the ages of 30 & 45 with two children & a household income of $50,000 who rent their home, have money or credit, "issues" are encouraged by retailers like Wal-Mart to shop at a super center that "has it all." Wal-Mart targets audiences that are on a budget but are also concerned with time & being able to find everything they need without driving all over town. Wal-Mart's slogan is "Low prices – everyday."

Men & women ages 55 or older who are married with a household income of over $100,000 a year, & who are physically fit are encouraged by Carnival Cruise Lines to take a "dream vacation." Carnival offers luxury cruises to exotic destinations while providing rest & relaxation on a "fun ship". "The most popular cruise line in the world" employs celebrity spokeswoman Kathie Lee Gifford to appeal to their demographic.

By learning how to define demographics you are one step closer to delivering a heartfelt voiceover. Researching advertising trends & demographic based marketing tactics will also help you to better understand the needs & motives of advertisers. Gaining a broad range of knowledge when it comes to advertising, regardless of your personal interests & buying habits will prove helpful when dealing with your clients. After all, most all retailers in any given industry want the same thing. For example – local car dealers want to sell their new & used lot inventory. Most of them go about it in a similar manner.

You must become a student not only of voiceovers but of advertising and the psychology behind it. Start paying *very* close attention to radio & TV ads as well as print media, billboards, and other forms of outdoor advertisements. The next exercise will help you identify & effectively communicate with different demos which will also help you to quickly and effectively assess the demographic a script is trying to reach.

LESSON #4: DEMOGRAPHICS PART 1

Make a list of 4 *completely* different people in your life & define their demographics by analyzing their lives. Write a problem or issue that you need to talk about. Use the same topic for all four people.

Consider how you would speak to these individuals about your problem & how each will react & what they may say. You want their approval, their forgiveness or help. In order to get it, you have to handle this matter "the right way", which will change with each person. You have a specific motive. In order to manipulate the outcome – you must be calculated in your actions. Don't just pretend, make the call. Let the person know you are "role-playing". Don't tell them why, just ask them to play along.

Goal: To understand how people change behaviors & speech patterns based on who we are interacting with. Your goal is to persuade an audience, to touch people on an emotional level by speaking to their demographic needs, wants & expectations.

LESSON #5: DEMOGRAPHICS PART 2

This exercise will help you identify & effectively communicate with people in your demographic.

Write a list of the products & services that appeal to you. What advertising affects your buying decisions? Did those companies speak to you in some way?

Then pay close attention to a few hours of radio & TV commercials & see if you can easily identify who the target audience is in each commercial. Some might be harder than others, but by & large, if the commercial is a good one you'll know very quickly who the advertiser is trying to reach.

Goal: To define your own demo & analyze what current trends advertisers are using to speak to different groups of people.

Voice acting is best when you are able to psycho-analyze both your listener and your character. You do this by studying behavior, thought patterns, age groups, stereotypes and the other nuances of the human condition. We strive to be experts in Social Studies.

Reading Copy

Script copy is something you will have frequent exposure to as a voiceover artist. Copy is never the same twice. Its appearance, layout, & design change from source to source & industry to industry. Copy for a TV commercial often looks very different from radio commercial copy & narrations can come in any number of formats. So don't worry too much about what "real" copy looks like. You will however, soon notice, that there are some very predictable patterns to the way scripts are written.

Any type of text can be used to practice with & almost any text can be turned into a voiceover. Magazine article's and ads are particularly effective practice. Or use the scripts at the rear or this book. In this section you are going to learn many things and it all starts with the ability to site-read.

Site reading is a skill developed over time as you become more exposed to scripts. It's the ability to almost flawlessly deliver a piece of copy, on mic, that you've never seen before & that you have not pre-read. It's a talent's ability to "predict" what the copy will say & translate it into a great VO.

It's not as hard as it sounds. Copy shares a lot of common bonds, & there are universal truths that can be found in almost every script. VO talent learn these patterns over time & how to read ahead of themselves while speaking. It takes lots of practice to develop this "script-sense".

You can practice this technique simply by reading out loud as often as possible. Pick up a book or magazine & read & speak at the same time. The skill is necessary because talent usually do not have time to pre-read material they are voicing, especially if the job is large. Audio books & large narrations are nearly impossible to pre-read. Time just doesn't allow for it.

We are going to focus on some basic techniques for pre-reading copy. These techniques will help you to understand how a talent decides on a course of delivery & how they later develop these techniques into site reading, interpretation & ultimately, delivery of the copy.

Once you have a lot of experience with different types of scripts, you'll get a good feel for how to interpret them. The thing to remember is this: there is no such thing as a bad interpretation. No two professional voice people will ever read the same script the same way; neither interpretation is bad, but one may be better suited for the client or may be closer aligned with the client's vision.

Every piece of copy can be interpreted at least two different ways (sometimes a dozen) so; always have two or three courses of action ready. It only increases your chances of getting the job, especially if you are auditioning. No matter the interpretation you choose your goal is always to visualize the meaning of the material you are reading.

Copy reading basics are very universal, but are often overlooked by new talent. Here are the essential:

DO - SMILE: Most beginners don't smile nearly enough. A big brilliant smile on your face can truly brighten any piece of copy & make it shine.

Men for some reason have a harder time with this than women. It may at first seem awkward to smile all the time but if you don't believe what a huge difference it can make, try spending a whole day NOT smiling. You'll see how fast people ask if something is wrong - even over the phone.

DON'T - CLIMB LADDERS: When trying to build intensity or show a sense of urgency & excitement, many beginner talent will climb or descend the proverbial VO ladder.

This means you are allow your pitch to constantly go up, up, up, until you sound like Minnie Mouse on helium. And don't go down, down, down until you resemble Barry White. Don't become sing-songy (like a children's book) either. Instead pretend that there is a bouncing Karaoke ball in front of you. Watch as it bounces up & down in a random & unpredictable pattern. That is what you should be doing with your voice; mixing it up!

DON'T – Up-Talk: Up talking is a fairly new phenomenon in the American speech pattern. It is frequently heard in the voices of adolescent girls and young women in their 20s. It is a habit the speaker has adopted, whereby almost all of their statements sound like questions. When you mistakenly turn a statement into a question it makes you sound uncertain of your words. This can be problematic for a voiceover actor since we are expected to sound confident and sure of ourselves.

Speed and Tempo

New talent have a tendency to race through copy very quickly while performing. This is usually the result of nervousness and a certain amount of intimidation brought about by the microphone itself.

Invest in a stop-watch. Use it during practice time to clock and monitor the length of time it is taking you to read a script. Try your best to maintain a steady tempo that allows you to speak clearly and normally. If you find that you are speaking too quickly, use the stopwatch to help you adjust your tempo and slow down.

When people speak normally and naturally, they pause often. Those pauses lend to the conversational expectation of natural everyday communications. Do not feel obligated to fill every second with speech.

Many scripts are written to emulate natural speech patterns and natural pauses. A good rule to follow is that a comma, period or semicolon denotes a one-beat pause. (Pause). A colon, dash or exclamation mark represents two beats. (Pause, Pause). And an ellipsis, line break in the text, question mark or double dash represent three beats of pause. (Pause, Pause, Pause).

Broadcasters, radio disc jockeys and actors quickly learn that pauses are their friends. A pause offers you time to think and strategize your next line of copy. Pauses also create drama, anticipation, and believability.

If you perform at a fast pace, you will also make unnecessary mistakes. This will happen because you are not giving your brain, eyes, and mouth time to work together in order to read and formulate the right words. There is a coordination that must take place if you are to read and speak the right words at the right time. I call it "Eye, Brain, Mouth Coordination." It's an essential skill or muscle memory that builds up over time and with practice. This is the time it takes for your eyes to recognize a word; the time it takes for your brain to find the meaning in the words and the time it takes your brain to signal your mouth to form the proper word. You can't properly build this ability if you don't spend copious amounts of time reading aloud. Voiceover actors are professional readers and our vocabulary and reading skills must be excellent in order to succeed. In addition, if you read too quickly, it will be difficult to properly analyze and assess a script for meaning.

Don't worry too much about the time count noted in a script. At least not right away. The time count is for the final product – if the client has written too much copy, they may have to make the decision to cut some lines during the final recording session. For the purpose of auditions you should ignore time codes completely. Instead of worrying about the clock, you want to make certain that your performance is the best that it can be – and that usually requires taking your time.

Many talent find that when they race through an audition to meet a time code, the audition is horribly rushed and their acting skills suffer. When auditioning your goal is to 'win' the job by providing the best interpretation of the copy provided. That will be very hard to do if you are rushing to beat the clock. Don't even look at the clock when you're auditioning. Instead focus on your performance and character development.

Also, please understand that you're not in a race to get to the end of the script. Many new voiceover actors suffer from what I call 'microphone syndrome'. This happens when your nerves get the better of you. A little voice in your head tells you that your job is to read the words on the page & because you have a microphone in front of you and the words you must not stop talking until you reach the end of the script.

When you let this happen your VO becomes a runaway train. You rarely stop to breathe, (so you run out of air frequently), and your words have little meaning because you aren't focusing on what you are saying.

I frequently tell my students treat every script like a two-way conversation. TAKE YOUR TIME.
Pause for action.
Reaction...
and reflection by both you & the audience.
Doing so will result in a much more natural voiceover.

Is there such a thing as too much pausing? In today's digital, non-linear editing world, pauses, breaks and gaps in a voiceover recording can be tightened & reduced as need be. You could literally stop in the middle of a script, do the Hokie Pokie, turn yourself around (a few times) & then resume reading! That's how much time you actually have! Savor & enjoy it. The clock can be your friend. Don't allow it to become your enemy.

LESSON #6: INTERPRETING A SCRIPT

Define the answers to these questions with all scripts from now on.

How does the product "feel?" Somber? Cheery?

Make sure you understand the product or service & its intended use. If you are voicing numerous spots for a hospital, the spot for the pediatric & / or maternity ward will have a totally different feel from that of the Trauma Care Center in the Emergency Room.

When you read make sure your voice & tone reflect the right mood & attitude. Your sound must portray a firm belief in the product. Everything you say should be definite & strong, never wishy-washy or questionable. And since you won't always feel it, be prepared to fake it.

Who are you trying to reach?

Match the script to the right demographic. You will not read for Mitsubishi as you would Jaguar. You want your voice to grab the right people. So ask yourself who the consumer is. Think about how they live, work, & play. Then speak to them accordingly.

What's the benefit to the audience?

People do not buy based on statistics, facts, pie charts, & graphs. They buy something because of how it makes them feel or how it will make them appear to others.

"The V6 Vortec, 264 horsepower, turbo charged engine with dual track suspension" doesn't sell a car. But "the wind in your hair as you roll with the top down, making you the envy of the neighborhood in your new convertible" *feeling* does. People buy benefits. If we all bought things based on what was actually "the best", think about how many frivolous purchases we would avoid!

Here's a quick advertising formula to keep in mind when using this lesson: Everyone wants the S.A.M.E things.

S>A>M>E> Security-Authority-Money-Ego.

LESSON #7: SCRIPT ANALYSIS

Transcribe a commercial from the radio, TV or internet. Use a magazines ad or select from the practice copy in this book.

Define your character & give it life. Even if you are reading as an announcer, you must give purpose to your voice. Are you rough & callous, or kind & caring? What will the feel of your read be? Prepare to perform all options if there is more than one.

Use your hands, face, your whole body – get into it! Act out your part. Credibility & authenticity are crucial. Do whatever it takes to make the copy real. If you physically use your body, your voice will follow. This means you must *move* on-mic. Voiceover actors don't stand still with our arms crossed when we perform. We dance, shake, shimmy, wiggle, talk with our hands, gesture, and interact with the imaginary friends only we can see and hear.

Talk one-on-one to someone you know. Remember you have a particular audience in mind. But you are always speaking as though you are talking to one person. Picture your intended demographic & speak as if someone you know who fits that mold is in the room.

Ad-lib your way to a great read. You can ad-lib your way into a read. People are noisy. We communicate with laughter, sighs, even a moan. Don't be afraid to go "off the script" & add subtle sounds that will enhance your believability. An "ummm" can do it! If you see the need, add little things to the script that will enhance its credibility & make your voiceover all the more real. A well placed laugh, a groan, a moan, a sigh or a little stumble, or trip-up in your words might be all it takes. But whatever you do, DO NOT alter the copy or change the words of the script at all. Many client's have legal departments that approve and scrutinize copy before it gets to you. If you change the words, even a little, the material may need to be resubmitted to legal, which can cost the client a lot of money. As a result many clients are very protective of a scripts "structural integrity".

LESSON #8: COLORING

New talent spend too much time focusing on their voice & too little time focusing on the words in front of them & the impact those words should have on the listener.

Choose a piece of copy. Identify the words that can be made to sound like what they mean; these are your color words. **"Easy"**, **"beautifully"**, **"warm"**, **"soft"**, **"tiny"**, **"comfortable"**, **"huge"**, **"up"**, **"down"**, **"pretty"**, and **"ugly"** are just some of the words that should be read in a way that conveys their meaning. Underline them, too.

Whenever you see the word "carefully", in a commercial, as in: "We carefully manufacture all our products…" you should read the word with CARE. Put stress on adjectives by:

- slowing you pace and or tempo on that particular word

- elongating the word and s-t-r-e-t-c-h-ing all or part of it.

- or speeding the word up

- making the word move or dance – give it rhythm

Pay close attention and you'll find that people do this in normal speech to make stories more interested and to paint a clearer picture for whomever we are speaking to.

Now practice reading the copy & make your colors words stand out or pop. You want to be careful not to emphasis the words simply by getting LOUDER. Don't yell; or punch the word, instead, make it interesting. Use tempo to add flair to these words by elongating or quickening the pace at which you say them.

View the underlined parts not as words but rather as emotions on the page. Repeat this exercise with at least three more pieces of copy before continuing on.

Goal: To add emotion and meaning throughout a script.

LESSON #9: CREATE AN ON-MIC ENVIRONMENT

Creating an environment on-mic requires the use of mic and vocal techniques as well as the proper analysis of a script. There's much we can do to create a sound experience that would make the listener believe we are somewhere other than a recording studio. Use the following practice copy to try each of these techniques:

Over a pot of chocolate, conversations go much longer than 140 characters. Welcome to the fondue effect - The Melting Pot - book your reservation at the melting pot.com

Intimate

An intimate setting requires you to use the same volume and tone of voice you would use if you were very, very close to someone while engaged in an intimate or private conversation. It's hushed but not a true whisper.

This environment also requires you to get very close to the mic, treating the mic as if it was someone else's ear. The resulting sound is very rich and full and tricks the listening into thinking you are very close to them physically.

This technique can also be thought of as pillow talk or among adults or the same tone a parent might choose to calm a hysterical child. It's calming, genuine and controlled.

Whisper

Telling your audience a secret or something for "their ears only" can be a very powerful method. This is reserved for moments when you want the listener to believe you have information that is juicy gossip that you're only willing to share with them.

Take a moment to actually whisper the copy. This will not work on mic. It is simply to soft and too inarticulate. Instead you learn to employ a "mic whisper" – your voice is pulled to the back of your throat, removing any bass as you constrict your vocal chords. But you do not decrease your volume. You are in-fact, fully audible to everyone in the room. However you add the same urgency and slow pace that you would to a whisper while getting very close to the mic. This allows the listener to understand just how important your message is. Give it a try.

This technique is similar to when a mother scolds her child in public. Despite her best efforts to keep the moment private, Mom might be so frazzled that her warning (although hushed) still comes out much loaded than she anticipated.

Yell

Much like a mic whisper, a mic yell requires some specific mic and vocal techniques. First yell, really yell – as if you are in a large crowd and competing over a lot of noise to be heard.

On-mic you'll need to reduce your over-all volume while backing away from the mic in order to avoid over-modulation. You aren't really yelling, so much as you are loudly OVER-ARTICULATING-EVERY-THING-YOU-SAY. You want to give the impression that you are competing with a lot of other noise and you can't really hear yourself. It sounds very similar to the way the elderly and hard of hearing speak all the time.

This technique requires a lot of imagination. Hear yourself talking over, a nearby train or plane, a lawn mower, a jack-hammer, horribly loud music or some other decibel increasing nuisance.

If we never strive to create varied environments and special differences in our recordings, then everything we do always sounds the same; one note if you will. This is limiting for a voiceover actor and one of the ways in which a beginner can be denoted among professionals with more experience.

LESSON #10: FINDING THE FUNNY

Copy and script writers think they are hilarious. No, really. They are the funniest people they know. Everyone from the novice writer to the pro, believes they are super witty and awesomely clever the moment they put their fingers to the keyboard. Occasionally you will find a legitimately witty and humorous script. Usually they are peppered with bad puns and mediocre jokes.

Regardless, you are the voiceover actor must 'find the funny'. Script writers try their hand at little bits of humor so frequently that you have to be on the lookout for it in your scripts.

These little moments of humor require you to be "in on the joke," otherwise they will fall flat and not meet the intended delivery.

Find the funny in the sample copy provided below.

When the Internet started, some people were like, this is stupid. Real surfing is better. But others were like, wow, these cat videos are hilarious! Be like that second group. Bury your bias and see the possibilities of our creamy, sweet tanginess, and what it can mean for your sandwich, and your future. Keep an open mouth. Get a sample at facebook.com/miraclewhip

You know how to cook. Your golf game is in the bag. And you've got killer dance moves. You think you're doing everything right. Bottom line, you're well rounded. Except for one thing. Bet you're not cleaning out your fridge often enough. In fact, 70% of Americans over the age of 25 only clean their refrigerators twice a year. A fresh box of baking soda won't cut it. You need full purge and wash down at least once a month. So break out a new sponge and some soapy hot water and clean up your act. Then take a breath. And get back to being all that on the dance floor.

When looking at a piece of copy, you must pretend that the experience in front of you is your own. You always begin with yourself. If you have a hard time loosening up in front of people or you worry a lot about feeling foolish or awkward when showing emotions in front of strangers, you must get over that fear. Practice is key & getting comfortable with your own voice is essential.

Emotions are personal; you yourself must have experienced an emotion in order to explain how you feel to someone else. You can't teach someone how to tie their shoes if you've never done it. In the same way, how could you define or convey anger if you've never known it?

Emotions really only serve one purpose; spoken or otherwise, our emotions convey to others how we feel. Emotions are contagious and a genuine emotion can alter how another person feels. But here's an interesting question -- does how we interact with others affect how we convey our most basic emotions?

Well, let's talk about love for a moment. Would you express your love for your mother the same way you would for your spouse? I hope not! Here's another example: if you needed to borrow money you probably wouldn't approach your great-grandmother the same way you would your best friend. Because people are individuals, we treat them & interact with them differently based on expectations.

A voice talent must understand the expectation of the audience they are speaking with. You must treat every performance as a two-way conversation, not a single sided one. Depending on who you choose to speak with, it can greatly alter the direction of the conversation and your social expectation at the time.

Every conversation is an opportunity to manipulate a group or an individual. Even if your goal is to be likable & credible; you will alter your words and demeanor to make yourself appear to be – likable and credible.

LESSON #11: STORYTELLING

Storytelling is based on the relationships that humans have with one another. A great story can make you laugh or cry but it will always make you *feel* something.

A voiceover person is not just reading & conveying words. You can't just speak for the sake of hearing your voice. Anyone can do that. The true measure of a voiceover artist is his or her ability to make others *feel*.

Read the stock report to an infant in a soothing voice & you'll lull him (or her) to sleep in comfort. Read the sports pages to a baby in an excited & goofy tone & you'll make him (or her) laugh. The words on the page don't matter. Your style of delivery does.

Take an article from the newspaper or a magazine.

- Perform it as if it is something very funny.

- Do it again as if it's traumatic news.

- Again, as though it's a children's fairy tale.

- And finally, read it in an alluring or sexy manner.

Don't just do it one time either – work on perfecting each of these of reads.

Make sure you are confident in their effectiveness.

Can you add others? Try a few ideas of your own. This is an exercise that you should revisit often and practice many, many times.

Goal: To make others "feel" an emotion and understand your state-of-mind. Also, to begin focusing not on how you sound but instead to focus on the scenario you are creating. Sound will not help you, scene will.

LESSON #12: EMOTIONS & FEELINGS

Below is a list of emotions & feelings:

Content	Pleased	Ecstatic	Glum	Numb
Miserable	Annoyed	Hostile	Puzzled	Timid
Tense	Frightened	Fatigued	Vulnerable	
Confident	Offended	Doubtful	Stressed	Aloof
Preoccupied	Wary	Overjoyed	Indifferent	

Pick one word to start.

Glean from all sources in your life & really think about the most Annoyed you've ever felt. Think about friends & family as well & their experiences with the same emotion.

Think back to your past. When have powerful emotions affected you? Were they yours or someone else's? Was a moment so raw that it carried you away? Write that story down from a first person perspective, even if the story is not your own.

You don't have to explain why you feel the way you do, & the story doesn't need to be in sequential order. Don't worry about an ending either. If the story requires "colorful" language, use it. Let it be really, real.

Start writing & stop after 1 page and re-read it.

Does your mind totally agree with what's on the page or is a voice in your head correcting you? If you have any doubt that you have not been 100% real with your words, start over.

Continue & write a page for each emotion.

Goal: To see the power of emotions when telling a story.

Everyone has a voice inside his (or her) head. We're not talking about the voice that tells you to stay home & clean your gun. We're talking about your subconscious voice. Your subconscious is most directly connected to your true emotions. Often, during conversation, we censor our subconscious voice. Sometimes we do it to spare others from hurt feelings, or perhaps, to keep from embarrassing ourselves.

Every now & then our emotions become so strong that our censor shuts off. You might be terribly embarrassed afterward. But there can also be something very gratifying about telling someone what you *really* think. Be it deliberate or accidental, that moment is as genuine an experience as we can have as human beings.

At some point in our lives, we encounter a person whose internal censor is naturally shut off. Sometimes we wish these people would learn how to turn it on! We call them "shameless" or "ruthless" or worse yet, "insane" if we were offended by them. We call them "crazy", "eccentric", "wacky" & "immature" if they are our friend.

Admire those folks for a moment & realize that they live their day-to-day lives controlled by their raw emotions. They are quite possibly the most "real" people you'll ever meet. They speak their mind. A collegiate study recently determined that people who liberally use cuss words & vulgarities in their speech are more honest and trust worthy than those who never curse!

These free-thinkers are not easily offended and they aren't easily embarrassed, as such, they exemplify some pretty desirable traits for voiceovers actors.

Take out your notebook & scan through a few of the pages you wrote in Lesson 10. Chances are you now have some really great scripts; the kinds of scripts that professional VO artists and actors live for. The types of scripts that give us the chance to step into the shoes of another person and tell their story. Your next lesson will put those scripts to use!

LESSON #13: ACTING OUT

This is an emotional exercise that will help you to "act out" any & every emotion at any given time by using what you wrote in Lesson 10. Find a quiet, isolated place & prepare to be loud! Also give yourself room. Room to wave your arms, stomp your feet, throw a pillow, or otherwise act outlandish. Now, pick one of the stories you wrote, take a deep breath & tell your story!

****

Did you "feel" your performance? Was it believable? If someone overheard you, would they have believed the emotion?

Do it again & really try to get into character; become the person telling the story.

Let it all hang out; cry, laugh, shout, giggle, moan, sigh, and do whatever it takes to make it real.

****

You know you've got it when you feel emotionally drained or when you've actually succeeded in scaring yourself a little. You might even end up crying or with an extreme case of the giggles.

Repeat this lesson with the rest of your emotional writings.

Repeat this lesson often with scripts that require extremely genuine performances.

Goal: To capture emotion in your voice & deliver a believable, emotional read.

LESSON #14: INTERPRETING EMOTIONAL OPTIONS

Go back to your written exercises from Lesson 10 & select one of the emotions.

Let's say you choose "disgust". There are many different ways to convey that feeling & all are very effective. Think of some alternate ways to deliver your story.

If you chose to *yell* your disgust for dust bunnies, now, try gritting your teeth & being quiet with your disgust.

Since every person displays emotions differently, you're trying to deliver this story in a way other than what comes naturally to you. Think of the people in your life. Some choose to shout when angered. Others get very quiet in a no-nonsense way when they get mad. Take a different approach & tell your story again.

****

Do you hear the difference? Do you prefer one delivery over the other? Which was a better performance? Which was more believable?

Jot some notes in the margin of your story's page & write as many ways as you can think of to tell that tale.

Revisit your other scripts & do this for all of them.

Variety is very important in VO. It's important to be a versatile performer that can deliver the same script in multiple styles.

Goal: To recognize & deliver all the different ways you can interpret a single piece of copy.

Inflection allows you to use your voice to make subtle changes to the mood & manner of your delivery. A great VO talent must be a master of inflection.

As with most of the skills needed for VO, we inflect all day, every day. This is nothing new to you. Every day our voices rollercoaster up and down nimbly as we speak to others. We hardly give the process a thought. In the course of a day, via nothing more than casual conversation, we change & alter our inflection dozens of times. If you are a very animated person, it might be hundreds of times a day that you change your inflection.

Because VO is a study in the natural & normal human patterns of speech we have to carefully analyze the expectations others have when we speak. If we all spoke like Ben Stein, no one would ever know if our words were genuine.

Catch phrases are a wonderful example of inflection at work. What makes a catch phrase catchy is the way it's said, not so much the words spoken. If we alter the inflection of a catch phrase, the results can be very disappointing.

When you shorten or elongate a word or syllable, frown or smile or change your pitch up or down rapidly you are using inflection to its fullest.

We've included some examples of well-known catch phrases. Analyze them, speak them out-loud & see if you can identify all the fine points of inflection that make each phrase unique. It's not enough to simply imitate the original performance. You want to really pick apart what makes the phrase memorable and catchy.

Yabba-dabba-do!	**Fred Flintstone**
How you doin'?	**Joey Tribbiani from**

Friends

That's Hot!	**Paris Hilton**
Quick, to the Bat-mobile!	**Batman**
Don't have a cow man.	**Bart Simpson**
Did I do that?	**Steve Urckle, Family**

Matters

What's up, doc?	**Bugs Bunny**
Here I come to save the day!	**Mighty Mouse**
Lucy, I'm home!	**Ricky Ricardo**
Luke, I am your Father.	**Darth Vadar**
Live long and prosper.	**Spock – Star Trek**

I'm gonna love you & squeeze you & lock you up in a little cage & call you George. **Gossamer - the big, red Warner Brothers monster**

What you talking 'bout Willis?
Gary Coleman - Different Strokes

I'll get you my pretty, & your little dog too!
Wicked Witch of the West—Wizard of Oz

One of these days…pow! Right in the kisser!
Ralph Kramden from The Honeymooners

LESSON #14: INFLECTION PERFECTION

A Great talent can take a single phrase or word & use different inflection to change the meaning, quickly.

Record the word "**Now**" to convey:
- A command or demand.
- Confusion.
- Irritation or annoyance.
- The prequel to a phrase, as in "now we will…"

Record the phrase "**Oh that's great**" to convey:
- Anger
- Shock
- Playfulness
- Extreme satisfaction
- Gratitude

Record the phrase "**It's a good deal**." to convey:
- A matter of fact. A literal statement.
- Sarcastically, it's in fact not a good deal.
- Wishy-washy, you're not convinced.
- Emphatically. You are trying to convince someone else that it is a good deal.

By now, you probably know or have realized that voiceover is a cousin to the acting profession. A great actor puts his all into his role; his body, his voice, his mind & his soul so that you believe his story.

Now imagine being an actor on stage...but no one can see you. They can only hear you. All of your audience's senses have been taken away but one. And somehow you have to put all the heart, soul & emotion of your monologue into your voice. That's what it means to be a voiceover person. Imagine trying to hug someone without touching them. It's difficult but it can be done.

Now, before this all makes you run for the hills mumbling about how you never wanted to be an actor, think about this: every day, start to finish, you naturally tell stories with friends, family, & co-workers. It's a part of your day-to-day routine. You already know how to do this! What you now need to do is harness that ability, fine tune it, & learn a few tricks of the trade to make it all come together behind a microphone.

Previous sections in this book have introduced you to what is known as the "art of acting natural". You're learning to take your natural, human, storytelling abilities & use them behind the microphone.

But to be truly prepared you have to be able to mimic even the not-so glamorous moments in life. What's your natural reaction to stubbing your toe? Or tripping & falling? Or having the hiccups? What you'll do & how you'll handle these situations in private is likely very different from how you'd handle them in public.

New voiceover people often make the mistake of trying to sound pretty or perfect in everything they do. Human beings by nature are flawed & our emotions effect how we sound in all situations. No one in real life ever sounds perfect 100% of the time. Voice actors, therefore, make an effort to sound (when appropriate) ugly. This allows you to be more believable & truthful when acting out a script.

The less-than-perfect sound is desirable. With voiceovers, you learn how to put it all out on the line, face embarrassment head-on & experience true emotional exposure. You'll learn how to be "real" in all scenarios. When you have mastered this the rewards in the voiceover industry are endless.

The key to acting natural is to be a great observer & a great listener. There are stories in everything & to capture an emotion requires that you be exposed to every conceivable emotion - & often. But the confines of your life may not offer a broad enough spectrum, especially if you are an emotionally reserved person. The solution to this problem is to reach beyond your own life, into the lives of friends, family, & acquaintances.

Capturing the emotions of others is easy. You simply mimic them! After all, imitation is the greatest form of flattery. You can literally borrow & steal emotions from others. It's not much different from retelling a joke someone else told you. When you tell the joke to another, you take ownership of it. In that moment, you are taking possession of that humor even though it wasn't yours to begin with. This ability is essential in a recording session. It's part of what great VO artists are talking about when they refer to "theater of the mind".

Whenever you take ownership of a story you are recreating events for someone else & allowing the story to unfold for them via your words. As a result almost every great character of fiction is born from someone's personal experiences with a real life character. Big personalities are hard to ignore & they are universally appealing because they command the center of attention.

You can learn to captivate an audience simply by allowing the crazy characters in your life to be your muse. Better still, allow that crazy character a chance to possess your body and mouth! Then the fun really begins.

Characters & Impressions

Cartoons are plentiful in our world. Most of us grew up fascinated with at least a handful of cartoons that we now consider to be classics & every generation has had an obsession with animation at some point & time.

For most of us, animation is the reason we became voice talent. If this has you nodding your head frantically in affirmation then this next section is for you.

But...we want to start by clearing the cartoon air. A lot of what you are about to hear is not going to be what you *want* to hear. In the info that follows it may sound like we are being harsh, mean, or downright pessimistic about cartoon & character voiceovers. We're not.

Know ahead of time that we're being brutally honest. There are many misconceptions associated with this part of the industry. We want to dispel those misnomers & help you set realistic goals for your voice career.

Not everyone is right for this type of work. We're not trying to deter anyone from pursuing character voiceovers, but we are trying to help you avoid costly & time consuming efforts that might not be right for you.

Cartoon animation work, video game VO & impersonations are a very advanced portion of the voiceover industry. These are not for beginners for a multitude of reasons. The competition is extremely fierce & you're not only competing with experienced & veteran voiceover talent; you're also competing with professional actors, comedians & celebrities.

This is a very exclusive club within our industry. Getting consideration for animation, or getting in touch with potential employers typically requires the work of agents & managers who have Hollywood ties. This crew works for you & leverages your outstanding reputation in the business to help you get consideration & auditions for such work. So odds are, if you have such people working for you, you're probably not reading a book for beginners. This area of the industry also requires the most overall talent, technique & experience.

There are plenty of people who spend their whole professional working careers as highly respected VO people who make a fantastic living but still never manage to acquire a coveted animation role. Therefore, in your case dear reader, you must learn to crawl before you can run because there is a long road ahead.

Most professional cartoon character actors are just that; namely, actors. They are working members of the Screen Actors Guild (SAG). Very few of these people consider themselves to be voiceover artists exclusively. To them voiceover character work is just a facet of their acting skills.

To really gain cartoon or animated feature notoriety, you need a good bit more acting ability than the average voice artist. On-camera experience, as well as improvisation & stage credits will likely be necessary for you to gain work.

It is also helpful to note that animation VO work is dominated by the same few people. Nancy Cartwright is an example. For those of you who don't know her by name, rest assured, you know her voice. Nancy is the voice of Bart Simpson on the long-running & award-winning Fox TV show, "The Simpsons".

Nancy is not only the voice of Bart; she is the voice of nearly a ½ dozen characters on that show alone. Her ability to disguise her voice is incredible & although she has worked very hard for all she has, the woman is blessed with a God-given talent.

She is also known for her work on "The Rugrats" & numerous Hanna-Barberra productions. We recommend visiting her website &

reading her books for an in-depth view into the life of a professional cartoon icon.

In the late '80s & early '90s, it was the height of Bart Simpson's reign. At one time, Bart (Nancy) had a hit song on mainstream radio! But Nancy is not alone in her success. Her co-star, Dan Castellaneta (Homer), & many other celebrity voices like Gary Owens, Mel Blank, John Ritter, Hank Azaria, Whoopi Goldberg & in more recent years Brett Walters, Tom Kane & Bob Bergen are just a few whose cartoon / VO careers are worth "getting to know."

How many people do you know who can imitate Bart Simpson? Can you? This is called an impression. An *impression* is defined as an imitation of an existing cartoon or "fake" character. An *impersonation* is the imitation of a real life person.

In the voiceover world, impressions & impersonations are not highly respected for a number of reasons, mainly because so many are poorly done. They also pay poorly & are not very sought after. Impressions are used mainly by comedians & radio DJs (more reasons VO people frown upon them).

The majority of the impressions & impersonations you hear on the radio have been created in-house by the radio station's staff – usually for a stubborn or ill-advised client who was steered in a poor creative direction. The talent used for these impressions are not paid extra money or freelance fees. This work is just part of their day-to-day job.

Occasionally, paid impression work does happen. Usually an advertiser is looking for a topical, political or pop culture figure that has recently been in the news. They are trying to capitalize on that topicality. But just because you can do an impression of an American Idol judge doesn't mean you will get *hired* to do so.

We are including a list of virtually worthless impressions & impersonations that many people make the mistake of including on a demo: Captain Kirk, Kermit The Frog, Jackie Gleason, Sam Spade (any detective really), Danny Devito, Joe Pesci, Scarface, Miss Piggy (& the rest of the Muppet crew), Darth Vader, The Honeymooners, Ricki Ricardo, Alf, E.T., Bugs Bunny, Foghorn Leghorn, Yosemite Sam, Mickey or Minnie mouse, Donald or Daffy Duck, Austin Powers, Dr. Evil, Arnold Schwarzenegger, Vincent Price, Bobcat Goldthwait, Jim Carrey, anything Monty Python, Woody Allen, Homer Simpson, Mr. Burns, Regis Philbin, presidents Reagan, Bush (either), Clinton, Nixon…etc.

Along with these, you can add: NY mafia accents, southern / "country" accents, French accents, surfer dudes & valley girls, & if you're a woman – little girl / stuffy kid voices.

These are all characters that have gone down in the history books. They are no longer cool or hip & most of them have just been done to death. People are sick of hearing them & everyone does them.

To give you an idea of how serious the distaste is…in a single year, we receive a demo a month composed entirely of all the impressions listed above. They are mediocre impressions & the demos all sound the same. So much so, you wouldn't be able to tell which voice talent was which had the demos not been labeled. And frankly, these demos are so embarrassing it's hard to understand why anyone would want to claim them. A well known talent agency we work with goes so far as to automatically toss these demos into the trash.

Now, we will say this: If you have the ability to be your own worst critic & can really be honest with yourself about your impression & impersonation skills; & you still believe you have something worth presenting to the world, then go for it.

Make sure the voices you feature are as current as possible or they must be, hands down, the most incredible imitation of (insert name here) anyone has ever heard. Make sure it's so close to the genuine article that it will make someone's head spin. Also, if you're originally from the South & your Southern accent is superb, use it.

It's not to say that after years of honing your craft you won't be the next Nancy Cartwright. But you must learn all the basics of "straight" voiceovers first. You must learn to use your natural voice in very acting-intense voiceovers before attempting to drastically alter your voice for the purpose of character work. However you can certainly start learning the basic skills needed to *create* a character.

The best character voices are the ones that are unique & original. Everybody loves something new, especially when it's funny. Character voiceovers are all about make-believe & using your imagination to give voice & life to a piece of paper. We're going to use a similar method to help you create original characters of your own.

Character voices are not usually "thunk-up" in an animation studio. It's quite the opposite. A pilot script is written. A cartoon is drawn & then given a biography based on the script. Then, voiceover talent & / or actors are called in for an audition. They are given the picture, bio, & script & asked to present how they interpret the character's sound.

You can learn to make your characters leap off the page. Anyone can do this, because you already have the basic skills necessary to create amazing characters!

The key to making characters leap off the page is to use your whole body. Animation actor & VO Coach Bob Bergen says; "physically play the character & the voice will follow". It's a simple but profoundly powerful statement.

Whenever you utilize your whole being to act out a part, you make it that much more real. You go outside of yourself & find a completely new "person" living inside you! Your words become so much more impactful because you are physically feeling what you are saying.

Do you talk with your hands or know someone who does? This is the same method at work. If you ask someone who talks with their hands to refrain from gesturing during a conversation, a piece of their personality is literally extinguished.

You need to feel free to move your body while on-mic. However, it's best to practice these skills off-mic first. This way, you will have a full range of motion to work with.

Character acting entails more than just dialog. Your character is doing something and you must identify the physical actions your part requires. Act out the process. If your character is running for his life then you better run (in place). At some point in the performance you should sound as though you are out of breath & being chased.

Character acting is exhausting, sweaty work. After only a few hours of recording, most animation actors are physically exhausted and mentally drained. It's a great workout.

Play, play and play some more. Despite all my doom and gloom set-up regarding characters, the goal is not to scare you away from them. You should play with voices, have fun, make goofy sounds and voices, practice accents and embrace the character process. It's only when you risk both failure and embarrassment that you achieve something truly great!

"Physically play your part and your voice will follow."

- Bob Bergen Voiceover Actor & The Voice of Porky Pig

Where did I put those spare parts? I know there's an extra torso around here somewhere. Let's see…oh I know; I put it in this Newt nest. I'll just reach in & grab it. Oh drat it's too slippery. Darn Newts & their slime. I need my torso.

I wasn't doing anything, I swear. I was just waiting for Farswog so we could go to the new space arcade. I don't know anything about your gum balls. Why would I take them? You better leave me alone. Besides so what if I did take them—what are you gonna do? Oh no, help!

Oh, I hate when the kids visit. They make a mess of everything! Know it all little brats. Well I'll show them. I may be old but I've still got some fight left in me. There…all finished the perfect little monster tamer. A human, on a stick! Now I just need something I can poke at for a little practice before the brats get here.

LESSON #17: BE THE CHARACTER

Think about the people in your life. Who is a natural born character? Maybe it's your mother-in-law, your crazy cousin Louie, your fifth grade teacher. Picture them in your mind. Scrutinize how they move, look, act, dress, & walk. It all plays a role in what makes them unique. It also directly correlates to how they speak.

Now, try imitating this person. Really get into it. Move, walk, talk & act just as they would & imitate their voice the best you can.

When you think you've got it, call someone who knows this person. See if they can guess who you are impersonating. If you've done a good job, they will immediately be able to identify who you are trying to be.

Goal: To capture the essence & eccentricities of a quirky person.

LESSON #18: CATCH THAT CHARACTER

This exercise will help you create an original character, from scratch. Find a picture in a magazine that leaps off the page – the wackier they are, the better. The picture should exude personality.

Write a biography for your character. Be sure to define them, leaving no doubts about who he (or she) is. What's their name? Where are they from? What do they do for a living? Answer these questions in first person & start by writing; "Hello, my name is_____".

Write the way this person would speak. Use slang & regionalisms to accentuate & over-exaggerate who they are. If this person is funny, snotty, snobby, etc., make sure it's apparent. Whatever defines them should be up front & easy to identify. Create a caricature with words.

Goals: To bring a character to life with words.

If you have trouble finding inspiring images use the ones below to help your character juices flow.

LESSON #19: MULTIPLE PERSONALITIES

Use the character "bio" you created in Lesson 16 as a script & give you character life.

Make this person part of your life for a week. How would he (or she) react to certain situations? How would he (or she) feel about the weather, political or the new Liza Minnelli CD?

Do this in the privacy of your home, or in the company of very understanding friends & family members!

The best audience for these types of character sessions is pets! Your dog & cat don't care how you address them as long as the food bowl is full. Other aspiring talent will be willing to play this game too & it's great practice.

Go so far as to sing the way this person might & perform chores around the house the way they would. Create a little voice in your head that says "what would Clive the Bee Keeper say about that?"

Come back to this exercises often & you'll have a head full of voices before you know it!

Goal: To create "mic-ready" characters that you can recall instantly and maintain vocally for a long period of time.

Your character dictates a script. The script doesn't dictate the character! This is why it's so important that you think creatively when building a character. However, the hardest part of character development is creating something from nothing. Staring at words on a page and building a personality with very little to use as a creative catalyst can be frustrating and disheartening

LESSON #20 : CHARACTER DEVELOPMENT GRID

A simple and great way to develop characters and take the pressure off of creating something 'from scratch' is to use a grid or cheat sheet. By turning the character building process into a *match game*, you can relieve much of the stress that comes with character creation.

Ask yourself questions like what is my character's physical appearance? What does the character's pitch, tone, pace, and laugh sound like?

Take this or a similar grid into the booth whenever you practice with character copy. Add more options to the grid often and expand the number of possible combinations you can create.

Physical Stance	Facial Expression	Sound of Voice	Quirks
AGITATED	TENSE	RASPY	SHAKY
SHY	WEARY	MONOTONE	LISP
INVASIVE	CONTENT	HIGH PITCHED	LOUD
FLIRTATIOUS	LOVING	EXCESS DICTION	SOFT
CASUAL	MISERABLE	SLURRED	BREATHY

Types of Commercial Delivery

It's time now to more clearly define the types of voiceovers used in advertising & show you exactly what is expected from you in their delivery. All commercial voiceovers can be classified into a few advertising categories. These categories dictate how you will read copy & perform. Often times you will be informed (ahead of time) as to which of these categories a script falls into but if you're not sure, it never hurts to ask the client what they are expecting from your delivery style.

Sometimes two styles of reads are combined to create a type of hybrid. This is very common & you will quickly learn how & when that technique can be employed. You need to learn the basics & continue to work with your variety exercises so that you'll always be prepared with multiple styles of delivery & inflection.

Announcer

An announcer read takes on many different roles in the VO industry. It's sometimes referred to as a "straight" read. It means that you are not a character or a "real" human being. You are a "disembodied announcer man/woman". You are supposed to be a voice of authority - making a sales pitch for the product or company. You are the expert, so to speak and you know all the facts and statistics.

An announcer VO requires your own natural speaking voice, not a character or impression, & you should be friendly but firm in your delivery. Announcer reads are usually not very personal, & your effectiveness lies solely in how well you utilize your voice during the delivery. You will find that most announcer copy is generic in that it talks to the masses. What is being said is either neutral to all demographics or it is specific to a core demographic, but it singles out no one. You are not necessarily speaking to a mom or a dad or a particular type of person. You are trying to reach everyone who might have an interest in the product or service.

These are some examples of generic announcer copy:

- Excedrin Tension Headache: the headache medicine.

- McDonald's: we love to see you smile.

- The JCPenny store-wide sale is going on now.

Each of these lines can be delivered in a variety of ways. Because an announcer read does not usually have a specific pre-determined delivery, it's up to you as the talent to provide a variety of different presentations. You are expected to sound as if you really care about the product or company being sold. You are expected to reach the audience with the intended information & make them understand what benefits await them.

You are expected to present a simple, clean, friendly delivery that gets the message across. Most often, when it comes to announcer reads, you will be hired for your own, natural speaking abilities. This is the read that truly sounds like "you" because that's what the advertiser wants; a very natural, very believable sound – something that can't be faked.

Don't be misguided by the many terrible examples of announcer copy that exist on radio & TV. Like any profession; there is the good, the bad & the ugly. You will encounter many voiceovers on a regular basis that are sub-par. You must be very critical of this industry while you are learning. Just because an announcer decides to sound phony doesn't make it right. But in the right situation, is doesn't make it wrong either. Just know that most of what you hear on the radio is likely going to be poor. Whereas the better examples to turn to will be on TV.

Announcer reads are often mislabeled by the client! Client's commonly label scripts as 'announcer' simply because they don't know what else to call the character they have created. Clients frequently lack the creative skills and acting skills needed to see the words on the page as more than just a message to be delivered by a nameless person. Commercial client's frequently lack the ability to express what it is they want the voiceover to achieve. They will provide too little or far too much detail regarding the script and how it relates to you as the performer. A client's inability to properly define their needs can negatively affect your performance if you let it.

Never assume that a script marked announcer *is* an announcer read. Instead read the entire script & determine if the read requires a more personal touch. If the script has a life & a personality that is more than what the average announcer would offer you must take it upon yourself to redirect the delivery style and use a performance that better matches their needs.

Today's announcer understands all this *and* that less truly is more. In years past announcer performances required a saccharinely sweet, overly happy read with a way, way too big Erik Estrada-like smile. That's not the case anymore. Modern announcers are casual, understated, cool, calm and sincere. They don't go out of their way to try to make the audience happy because that's not the announcer's job. Credible and trustworthy is what most clients seek in an announcer today.

If you come from a radio background or if your voiceover dreams have been heavily influenced by radio *this* might be your hardest lesson. Broadcasters still tend to cling to the phony sound that leaves the audience feeling yelled at, verbally assaulted and or talked at. You'll probably need to really relax your delivery style to meet the needs of most modern announcer casting specs.

In today's non-announcer world of advertising the 'sell' is not longer the main focus of the material. The benefits of the product get all the attention while pronouns are understated or all-together disregarded. Words like 'you' or 'your' don't need to be hyped. The listener (the 'you') is no longer that important to the script.

LESSON #21: ANNOUNCER

This lesson teaches you to identify the different ways that announcer copy can be read.

This lesson uses the three announcer copy examples given on page 96. Read each one in 5 completely different ways.

It's easier than you think. Just take a moment to reflect before you inflect.

Try one read that is very neutral, try one that is very happy, try one that's a little more somber, try one that is matter-of-fact – the options are seemingly endless.

These are called A,B,C reads, since you are reading the lines, back to back to back in difference ways. ABC reads are very common and occur in almost every single voiceover session. This method allows a client to get multiple, varying, rapid performance options from you for a line, phrase, tag or statement.

Look at each line & decide on what delivery methods you think would work best. Determine why they work well with the advertiser & then read each one in the different styles you decided upon.

Can you hear the difference in your reads?

Goal: To be able to quickly & effectively determine five or more ways to read announcer copy.

In the past announcer performances required a saccharinely sweet, overly happy read with a way, way too big Erik Estrada-like smile. That's not the case anymore.

Hard Sell Deliveries

Hard sell is a generic term that refers to a style of delivery. Hard sells can be aggressive, in-your-face, energetic, stern or even fear inducing. A hard sell is not necessarily defined by the words on the page but more so by how a talent is directed to read it. Excess use of exclamation points can indicate a hard sell.

Hard sell tactics are pretty easy to identify based on their name. Hard sell is a harsh approach to selling. The copy is usually high energy, & creates a sense of urgency. Like all advertising there is good & bad use of this technique. Hard sell is most often identified by bad usage. Think about local car dealer ads. They are loud, obnoxious & often times the announcer is yelling or being extremely aggressive. Even though this is the most common use of hard sell; it is not the best use.

If at all possible, you want to avoid, alienating your audience by yelling at them. However many a misguided client will request this sort of read. On a national & regional level, you find these spots in conjunction with sporting good products, travel, concerts, & what can best be described as "male" products & services.

The advertiser is usually trying to leave the audience with a rush that appropriately matches the feeling you will walk away with after having partaken in a particular activity. Products geared toward young boys take the same approach. Action figures, play sets, & the like; have a "rough & tumble" feel.

This is active advertising so the goal is to motive the audience to do whatever the ad prompts. Usually this is to go to a website, call a number, go to a store or purchase something right now!

Hard sell advertising usually employs men but certain trends in the industry now require qualified women to deliver hard sell reads as a female voice will be more appealing to a primarily male audience in certain instances.

LESSON #22: HARD SELL

This lesson will help you identify key selling points of hard sell copy. Your believability is extremely important with hard sells because your energy level must match the tone of the product, & you must be very aware of the language being used to support it. Examples of such copy are:

THE PLACE YOUR MAMA WARNED YOU ABOUT!

GET READY TO GET EXTREME.

DO YOU WANNA GET ROCKED?

THE TIME TO BUY IS NOW!

Review each of these lines & think about the power & action in all of them. Practice reading the lines above & try to capture a true sense of urgency with each.

This is an edge of your seat, tense body and muscle, fast paced delivery.

Goal: To present a read that will cause your audience to take action.

———————————————————

Hard sell can be interpreted in many different ways. You want your audience's involvement in some way & you are appealing to a specific action or activity in their life. This is not passive advertising.

Some talent never master the art of hard sell. It's not everyone's forte & that is ok. But you should be aware of your own limits & what you are capable of.

The language & phrases used in hard sell spots are not typically found in anyone's day-to-day life because hard sell is used to grab attention. You need to know who your audience is & prepare a read that is so "larger than life" that it reaches right through the radio or TV, grabs them by the collar & shakes them – vigorously!

LESSON #23: HARD SELL PART 2

This lesson will help you to use your voice in the most powerful manner possible.

Spend some time identifying both good & bad uses of hard sell advertising on radio & TV.

Select a piece of hard sell copy from any source you choose.

Read the script in three of the following ways. Not all of them may be appropriate for the script you have chosen, but each is a type of hard sell read:

ANGRILY

SARCASTICALLY

SCARILY

AGGRESSIVELY

MALICIOUSLY

INTENSELY

AUTHORITATIVELY

CREEPY

In order to capture each of these deliveries you must find a source of inspiration for the read. Think of someone who embodies each of these words. Your favorite movie or TV villain is a great place to start.

Goal: To harness the range of delivery in hard sell VO that goes from very aggressive & energetic to calculating & intense.

Soft Sell

Soft sell, as we're sure you can guess, is the exact opposite of hard sell. It's a softer, more subtle way of delivering a message. Soft sell takes a slice of life & over-dramatizes it by tugging at people's heart strings. These are emotional reads that can make someone cry or smile. They make you feel cared for & they are extremely relatable.

Soft sell typically appeals to a female audience. Think everything from baby wipes to grocery shopping. They speak to a human's need for security & protection. Everyone wants to feel safe, cared for, & protected. You as the talent are playing the role of sympathetic adviser, or friend. Examples of soft sell commercials are companies like All-State Insurance, Gerber Baby Food, cosmetic surgery centers, & the tear-jerking coup-de-gras – On-Star.

Soft sell can be tricky because it requires that you not only sound as though you really care about the product or service, but that you care about the audience & their needs as well. You are breaking down barriers & talking to people about the things that matter most to us all - home & family. Your believability is critical to the success of the campaign. You are still the voice of authority, but now you are also the voice of reason.

Every voiceover talent, male & female, should be well-versed in how to deliver an effective soft sell commercial. Even if you don't relate to the product or service, you must sound as though you do. Sensitive subjects such as life, death, drug rehabilitation, illness, unemployment, medical care, and credit problems require finesse. These are sensitive subjects & you are appealing to these sensitivities on a very human level.

Your technique should entail a softer, more caring use of your voice –whispering or sounding a bit sheepish can turn a good soft sell into a great soft sell because these reads require empathy and humility.

Soft sell is typically low energy & you're not usually asking the listener to take a strong physical interest like you are with a hard sell.

Also, soft sell is more passive & speaks from an intellectual standpoint. You are *recommending* or *suggesting* that they try your product or service, not insisting. Likewise soft sell tactics don't expect or demand immediate action. The spot and delivery are asking you to consider a specific product, service or retailer the next time you are in need of that particular item. This is a 'slow and steady wins the race' approach to advertising.

Audience benefits are important too because you are asking people to make a change & break out of their normal routine. So you really need to emphasize the positive points & *benefits* they will obtain by using or buying the product or service your ad promotes.

Today's soft sells also include a form of non-selling. A type of ad that is so nonchalant, it isn't trying to sell you anything at all! Younger audiences are very turned off by obvious or overt selling methods. So many of today's top advertisers are opting for very understated, low-key performances. Simply put, we don't sell or 'pitch' our friends. Instead, we suggest or recommend things to them.

In most instances you can 'fake it until you make it' with soft sell, as the product or service you are promoting may not have an emotional connection for you. This is where your acting training comes into play in a big way.

Whether a script be a hard sell or a soft sell, at some point you will encounter a read that requires a sound that simply isn't 'organic' to you. If you find it hard to relate to the words on the page or the scenario being created, you may want to consider passing, especially if it's an audition.

All voiceover actors have something of an obligation to know and understand exactly what types of rolls they are well suited for. There's no shame in passing on a script if you're having trouble connecting with it. Every day, working professionals sort through dozens of scripts and audition opportunities in order to find and select the ones that are best for them. You may occasionally audition for something that you know is a long shot, but you should try to avoid making a habit of it.

Instead, choose the scripts that are right for you – the ones that look as if they were made or written specifically for you. Those are the ones you have the best shot of booking, especially when you can read it and know that the client would be a complete idiot NOT to hire you!

Soft sell requires that you not only sound as though you really care about the product or service, but that you care about the audience too.

You are talking to people about the things that matter most to us all - home & family. Your believability is critical.

To achieve a great soft-sell name three reputable spokes people / celebrity endorsers who are credible to you:

_____

_____

_____

LESSON #24: SOFT SELL

This lesson will help you deliver effective, believable soft sell reads. Spend some time identify soft sell advertising on radio & TV. Then, choose a script to work with from the sample copy in back of this book. You'll read the script multiple ways, while emphasizing primary selling points.

Read the script in three of the following ways. While not all of them may be appropriate for the script you have chosen, each is a type of soft sell read:

BUBBLY
SYMPATHETICALLY
CARINGLY
HOPEFULLY
SOOTHINGLY
EASY-GOING
MATERNALLY or PATERNALLY
LOVINGLY
HUMBLY
DISCRETELY

In order to capture each of these deliveries you must find a source of inspiration. Your favorite movie or TV parent will probably do the trick. Or everyone's best friend, a Jennifer or a John! Use Jennifer Aniston, Jennifer Gardner, or Jennifer Hudson as an inspiration. Guys can choose from John Cusack, John Goodman, John Travolta, or Jon Voight.

Goal: To harness the range of delivery in soft sell VO that goes from happy-go-lucky to loving to somewhat irreverent.

Testimonial

Whenever you're called upon to deliver a testimonial read, you should be proud. Testimonials are a true test of an actors skills.

A testimonial is a real-life read, meaning you are being asked to read as though you are a real person telling a tale or recounting a particular event or moment from your life. It's a first person account with an opinion.

Whenever the copy says "So I…"; "Then we…"; "My Husband & I…" it is a testimonial read. You are being asked to mimic real life in the confines of an advertising script. The 'I', 'Me', 'Mine', aspects of the script denote a vested, personal interest in the material.

National & regional advertising campaigns use testimonials as often as possible because they are very powerful & effective. Countless companies use them. When a well known celebrity records a testimonial, it's called an endorsement. The advertiser is trying to appeal to the audience on a very personal level by presenting them with a person, a situation, or a story to which they can relate.

Credibility is critical when performing a testimonial. If for any reason the audience does not believe what you are saying, the product will suffer & it's unlikely the advertiser will ask you to come back for another job.

Testimonials can be funny, sad, extremely happy, aggressive or angry; the emotional spectrum is endless! If humans have experienced it, it will appear in testimonial advertising. You're looking to strike a chord with the listener & make them understand that X product or service really does understand you & what you're like. And here's the proof – we've found someone just like you to tell you all about it!

The general public rarely realizes that these "real people" are paid actors. Even children are used in testimonials. If a client believes they can benefit from a testimonial read, they will use it. The hardest thing for a voice talent is learning how to deliver these types of scripts without sounding like a voiceover talent! You do not want to be mistaken for a paid professional; you are not the voice of authority or reason, you are just a real person telling a story about you & your experiences. That's all.

Most new talent spend so much time focusing on how to sound professional by controlling their tone & diction that they forget how to sound "normal". Beginners, untrained actors, and broadcasters work so hard to sound polished and professional. They are doing so because they think it's what's expected of them or because they still have a preconceived notion of what a voiceover actor sounds like. The truth is voice actor sounds like everyone else. The notion that we all speak perfectly and 'better' than everyone is something of a misnomer, or rather, an outdated view. The polished announcer of yesteryear doesn't have much of a place in modern voiceover.

Most commercial voiceover actors are hired because they can sound just like anyone else. They act naturally in front of a microphone and speak directly to someone they know in a way that is setting / situation specific. The actor turns every script into a two-way conversation. And a genuine read is a less-than-perfect read. Sometimes the only real polish that you show on-mic is your technical training, in-so-far as you know and understand how to best use the microphone.

Don't lose sight of being a layman in the world of VO. You will someday be asked to apply all your knowledge of the industry to go back to the point you are at right now & deliver a voiceover as "man on the street".

And please don't strive for perfect. As we all know, there's really no such thing anyway. And should your training, past experience or just natural abilities have already helped you to achieve a very polished sound, don't despair. There are loads of voiceover applications that will honor and respect that polish. Testimonials just aren't one of them. In order to achieve success in testimonials you'll need to be willing to 'muddy' your read and play a very casual character.

LESSON #25: TESTIMONIAL

Watch TV interviews on the news as well as talk shows that feature lots of "regular" guests. Focus on how guests tell their stories & write down words & phrases that stand out as "real". Practice reading the following phrases as well as ones you have written down.

please note that in today's day of texting and email communications many students become confused by script case text. It's very common to see scripts written in ALL CAPS. It does not denote yelling, an angry tone or any other form of dissatisfaction.

I LOVED IT!

I'LL NEVER DO THAT AGAIN!

I DON'T WANT THIS TO HAPPEN AGAIN.

YOU'RE THE BEST!

THANKS FOR BEING SO GOOD TO ME.

I KNOW…YOU THINK I'M CRAZY – RIGHT?

OH MY GOD – DID YOU SEE THAT?

EXCUSE ME, I'M SORRY, PARDON ME.

I'M SORRY I'M SO TIRED. IT'S BEEN A REALLY LONG DAY.

Pay special attention to questions. In any read, (not just testimonials), you must have the ability to pose a question naturally. You must sound as though you legitimately expect an answer from your unseen audience. Allow for a small pause, the same way you would if talking to a friend. Even rhetorical questions need pause.

LESSON #26: FIVE QUESTIONS OF ANALYSIS

Ask and answer the following questions with every script.

1) Who Am I?

You can be absolutely anyone you want to be. Let your imagination create every detail about your character. The only rules are: you can't be *you* and you can't be a salesperson or company representative. You must also maintain your gender and general age range.

2) Who Am I Talking To?

A neighbor, a friend, a family member…it can be anyone, but you must define this person too. The more details the better. You can even use a real family member or friend.

3) Where Am I?

Location is critical because it changes everything about the way we speak and what is socially acceptable. We speak differently in church, at an intimate setting like a romantic dinner, or at a funeral. Likewise our sound changes at a baseball game, a crowded bar, or if we're on a busy city street. Location matters a whole lot.

This is another way to create the environment of the copy which you learned in a previous lesson.

4) What Am I Physically Doing?

Whether you talk with your hands or not, we all naturally multi-task when we speak. We're cooking, cleaning, checking email, watching TV – all while talking to others. If you physically engage yourself in an action (improv style) in the booth, you're more likely to sound natural.

5) What Are My Motivations?

Motives are usually selfish. So think the worst and determine why your character is speaking in the first place because most people don't speak unless they have a reason to. Something has to benefit them.

Commitment is critical to analyzing your script. The answers to your five questions can't be wishy-washy – they must be defined and certain. You have to commit to your idea and follow it throughout the performance to the end. Be strong in your choices; bold even, and know that your listener can hear both weakness and uncertainty in your story.

One changed detail in your analysis can change your story completely.

Changes and choices allow you to better analyze your script and create optional or different approaches to the material.

Know what your choices are – but commit to only one at a time.

Make sure you are using your face to its fullest. The more expressive you are the more we can hear it in your voice. So put on your sad face, happy face, mad face, silly face, etc., and use it throughout the performance too. Practice in front of a mirror to ensure that your facial expressions aren't falling flat.

LESSON #27: CREATING BACK STORY

Back story, or the story *behind* the story recognizes a few really critical items with your script. Namely the fact that something had to happen before it!

Your script, every script, represents an encapsulated moment in time. An actor has to determine what happened before the first line of the script in order to understand the state-of-mind everyone is in, including their own.

There's no right or wrong ways to create back story. There are simply choices & the need to think creatively to build a scenario that fits the copy. If your back story doesn't exist your first line may always sound phony or stiff. Also without back story you lack the over-all connection with the words.

Read this example script:

"I guess I wasn't thinking. Chuck had been home, oh, a couple of months after doing two tours in Iraq. So now that Chuck was back, I wanted to make him feel at home again. And here's where I messed up. There was a new movie opening. And it was pretty violent. So I called Chuck to see if he wanted to go. And while we were watching, I could see he wasn't the same. But you know Chuck never talked about what he had seen or been through. And I didn't know the right way to ask.

Here are three separate back stories to go along with this script.

1) You are speaking with your therapist because you feel guilty.

2) Chuck's mom calls you and demands to know what happened at the movies. She is angry and you become defensive.

3) A close friend wants advice on what her brother will be like when he returns from a tour of duty.

Now, select another script & create 3 possibly back stories for it.

LESSON #28: BUILD A RAMP

Ramping is another common technique that helps voiceover actors to create a ramp or a launching pad for their script. Ramping requires that you build back story first.

Once you have determined your back story (we'll use the previous lesson to demonstrate) you create a mini dialog between yourself and the person you are speaking with to get you to your first line. It works like this.

Therapist: you seem really upset. Want to tell me what happened the other day?
You: I was an idiot and really messed up.
Therapist: How so?
You: I guess I wasn't thinking...

Chuck's Mom: What happened the other night? Chuck won't talk to any of us!
You: I didn't mean to upset him, it was just a movie!
Chuck's Mom: Just a movie! He's a mess and all you can say is that it was 'just a movie'.
You: I guess I wasn't thinking...

Sally: Hey so my brother comes home soon and I want your advice on what it's going to be like...
You: It'll be hard, he's not going to be himself at first. When Chuck got home I screwed up royally.
Sally: Will you tell me about it so I can avoid the same mistake?
You: I guess I wasn't thinking...

Practice using these ramps with the script from the previous lesson. Then chose a new piece of copy and apply both back story and a ramp. Your goal is to start seeing how a monologue can be transformed into a dialog.

LESSON #29: AD-LIBS

Adlibbing is an actor's dream. The ability to treat a script loosely & to interpret the words on the page as you see fit, probably sounds like fun right? Voiceover actors never get to do it! It's the script, the whole script & nothing but the script, so help us God!

However there is a form of adlibbing that voiceover actors get to use. Voice actors don't adlib words, we adlib NOISES. Long before there was language, people made noise. We yawned, sighed, giggled, guffawed, groaned and moaned just as we do today. Humans have always used noises to express our state of mind or state of being. Go anywhere in the word; (and despite language barriers) ever person knows that a yawn means you are tired or bored.

When we adlib noises into our scripts we create a genuine more realistic sound to our words & performance. A well placed laugh or snicker can make you really *real* to the audience. That is what clients want – a real, credible person.

Try it, select a script and strategically position a few well thought out non-word, noise adlibs. Write them into the copy if you need to – make little notations on the script. What often sounds spontaneous is actually premeditated.

Write down a list of noises that you commonly make. Then expand the list to include the noises of friends, family and strangers. Keeping a noise list will help you to select the best ones in studio.

This technique is so effective that clients hire a talent because of it and the clients can't figure out why! They will say things like, "Your audition was so much more real, so genuine, and you really stood out". It's adlibs that make this possible.

LESSON #30: SPONTANEITY

In addition to adlibs, there are a vast number of things that voiceover actors can do to sound real and spontaneous. Strive for an unpolished, imperfect, slouchy, less fluid read! I call it a 'dirty read' or finding your 'ugly' voice.

Too many voiceover actors strive for a polished perfect voice, yet so clients today don't want polished & perfect. If you have an acting background you're likely already a master of the technique. Here are ways to dirty a read, choose a piece of copy & try each.

- Elongate some of your thoughts. When we're not sure what we're about to say next, we wiiiiilllllll stretch a word as we grab for that next thought. This unscripted sound makes you way more believable. Script? What script?

- Try for a humble / vulnerable read with subtle disappointment. Humility and the occasional gripe are very normal. But those are not sounds the audience expects to encounter when something is being sold to them. The honesty in a humble delivery can really catch the listener off guard, as these 'flaws' make them forget they are listening to / watching an advertisement.

- Make every line of your script the answer to a question. Break your script down line by line and think about a possible question you could answer. It mimics natural conversation. Here's an example.

(Do you remember when you went to Pier 1?) *I remember the exact moment I decided to go to Pier 1.* (Where were you?) *I was right here, cleaning the kitchen, when I noticed that the only thing on my table, was a roll of floral-print paper towels.* (So what did you do?) *So I went to Pier 1 and got this great, fall candleholder and matching table runner.*

When Copy Goes Bad

Yeah, it's sort of like when milk is past its expiration date. Boy does it stink! Bad copy happens much more than professional VO talent would like. The problem is that copywriting is truly a neglected art form. Good writers are hard to find. And the really great ones have largely been laid off in favor of cheaper, untrained novices.

We live in an age of downsizing & multi-tasking. The advertising world has been devastated by these corporate money-saving tactics. As a result, we've seen an onslaught of horrible scripts over the last 10 years due to a lack of qualified, skilled writers. Sadly, there is no end in sight.

Bad copy makes a voiceover artist's job difficult. Run-on sentences, poor word choice, & grammatical errors can really make it difficult to get through a simple :60 script. Difficult, but not impossible.

Sometimes copy is so bad the voice artist is left wondering, "What are they trying to say in this script?" The message you are being paid to sell, the demographic being spoken to & your role in the spot may all be very unclear. So the question becomes, "What's a talent to do when bad copy happens?" The answer is simple. You must always remember that the copy isn't selling the product - you are. You are a breathing, feeling human being – the copy is just an inanimate object! When you find yourself in the booth with bad copy, focus on whatever positive points exist. For instance, no matter how bad a script is, you will always be able to find punch or color words within the copy.

Take time to identify bad copy on the radio, & bad VO performances. Learn from other's failures. Identify the problem areas, & ask yourself how you would correct it.

On the next page is an example of a poor script. Practice with it & apply the lessons you have learned in this book so that when you are exposed to a script like this, you will still give a consistently good performance.

Please know that all the misspellings, grammatical errors & poor wording in the script that follows is totally intentional. Yeah…we're doing this to you on purpose! In fact errors you find in all the scripts in this book are intentional. We have left them intact, exactly as they came from the client. We see errors in scripts everyday in this business.

ONCE AGAIN THIS YEAR MIKE'S TENT RENTAL IS HAVING A SALE. WITH SPECTACULAR SAVINGS EACH & EVERY ONE OF YOU PLANNING A WEDDING, CORPORATE EVENT, BACKYARD BBQ OR ANY OTHER OUTSIDE VENUE WILL BENEFIT. WHY NOT COME IN & SEE THE IMMENSE PRICE REDUCTIONS THAT ARE WAITING FOR ALL OF YOU? THERE ARE SO MANY OUTSTANDING VALUES NO MATTER THE OCCASION. FROM TENTS, TABLES, CHAIRS, DANCE FLOORS, & MORE MIKE'S TENT RENTALS WILL PERSONALIZE ALL OF YOUR PARTY NEEDS. YOU WILL APPRECIATE THE EXCELLENT VALUES AVAILABLE IN TENTED OPTIONS REGARDLESS OF WEATHER YOU MIGHT BE INTERESTED IN MOON BOUNCES, DUNK TANKS, SNOW CONE, COTTON CANDY, POPCORN, OR MARGARITA MACHINES FOR THE KIDS. YOU WILL QUITE CERTAINLY FIND PRECISELY THE CORRECT EQUIPMENTS TO ALLOW YOU TO PURSUE THE PARTY OF YOUR DREAMS. MIKE'S TENT RENTALS WORKS THE ENTIRE PROCESS SO YOU DON'T HAVE TO WHEN IT'S TIME TO PARTY OR TIME TO ENTERTAIN OR TIME TO IMPRESS, LET MIKE'S TENT RENTAL PITCH YOUR TENT & PERSONALIZE YOUR NEEDS. GIVE THEM A CALL 555-5555. THAT'S 555-5555. 555-5555 FOR MIKE'S TENT RENTALS.

Auditions & Sessions

Every performance exercise in this book has been designed to help you prepare for auditions. Auditions are the number one way in which talent obtains VO work. You perform to a client's specifications in order to show them a custom example of your skills. There are a number of factors that can help you land an audition & beat out the competition.

Make sure that you slate your audition with your name, the part you are auditioning for & the number of takes or versions of the material you are providing. Keep you slate quick & to the point; it should be no more than a few seconds.

Always provide more than one version of the material. Everything you have learned so far has helped prepare you to evaluate a piece of copy & determine multiple ways to perform the script. Providing a few options of varying inflections increases your odds of booking the job. It also helps the client to see that you are a thinking actor who is taking the time to consider alternate delivery styles. This sometimes provides a needed competitive edge, although more than three takes is overkill.

Never produce an audition. Submit the material dry without any music, sound effects or vocal effects. A client or the client's producer should be able to determine what additional production elements will work well with your voice. They need to be able to envision your voice as part of the final creation. By selecting production elements, you're taking control out of their hands. They may even produce a mock commercial from your audition. They can't do this if you've already done it.

Always follow the instructions given by the client carefully. A failure to follow instructions could result in your audition being disqualified. You don't want to be *that* person.

Save all audition copy & the audio you submit. It can take a client days, weeks or even months to make a final decision on a voice. A client may call months after your audition & say; "We loved what you did. Please don't change a thing from your audition during the final recording." That's going to be hard to accomplish if you don't have the original audition file to listen to & remind yourself of what in the world you did!

If you are asked to audition live & participate in an open (cattle call) audition, don't panic. Try your best not to be the first person to audition. You can learn valuable information from the performers that go before you. As they exit, simply ask them what the client is looking for. This will give you time to rehearse the copy in that manner before you are face-to-face with the director.

Ask the audio engineer or studio representative if you can sit in on the audition process as opposed to in the waiting room. This doesn't always work, but if they say yes, you'll have a bird's eye view of what your competition is doing & the feedback (if any) they receive from the client.

Once you are on-mic don't be shy about offering a suggestion to the client if you have a good idea as to how the copy might be performed. Most clients appreciate creative ideas. The worst they can say is, "no".

During your audition do not ask permission to retake a line or a phrase you did not like. If you feel you can do the line over & perform it better; just do it! Asking for permission gives them the chance to say no & stop the audition.

When your turn is up, thank everyone – offer a copy of your most recent demo & your business card & make a courteous but timely exit. Do not hang around. It's not appropriate to ask for an audio file of the audition. Instead, keep the copy if you can.

When an audition is complete, send it & forget it. Do not

obsess about the audition. Just let it go & let the decision-makers do their job. There is no need to follow-up or bug them about the status. If you book the job they will let be eager to let you know.

If you've never been in an actual recording session, it can be a bit daunting. When you are nervous about doing a good job for your client & out of your normal practice environment, it can be scary.

When preparing for a session away from home, bring items that you will need. A beverage, a light snack like fruit (oranges or green apples are best) & items to soothe your throat if it becomes overworked.

If you suffer from allergies, or any other respiratory problem, always have your medicine with you. You never know what might bring on an attack – you could end up blowing the session & losing the job if there's no time to reschedule. Oddly enough, allergens you never thought you'd encounter at a recording studio may be present. I've known many studio owners and studio employees who bring their pets to work; dogs and ferrets alike! One studio I work with regularly even has a resident studio cat.

If you're sick, let people know up front. There is no point in wasting anyone's time, especially if you're voice has been affected. Call ahead & let the studio know you're not feeling well. Let it be the client's choice to reschedule or continue as planned.

Warm up your voice on the way to the studio. Sing, hum or use your preferred warm up exercise to limber & stretch your vocal cords. Upon arrival; you'll greet the studio engineer & any client representatives. Ask to see the copy & the recording booth as soon as possible. You want to get situated & comfortable quickly. This will also, hopefully, give you a few moments to rehearse the material.

Make sure that any drink brought near studio equipment is in a re-sealable bottle or container. Most sound studios have strict food &

beverage policies & rightfully so. One accident & you could end up owing them thousands of dollars to replace damaged equipment. Never place a drink down near equipment or microphones. If you're not sure, ask. They'll show you where to put your drink. If all else fails, place it on the floor in a corner.

When everyone is ready for you to begin, *relax*, focus on your performance & take criticism & comments with grace. You know what you are there to do. Let your performance shine & have fun! Converse freely with the client and enjoy the moment. This is the magical part of our business.

When you are finished thank everyone & depart. Don't linger or hinder others from getting their work done. When you return home, immediately send an email thanking everyone again.

VO talent never stop learning. We all strive to continue our education indefinitely with the goal of always bettering our performances and our marketability. Every session, every piece of direction, every interaction is a chance to learn, to grow, and to better yourself. Even difficult clients present you with an amazing learning opportunity.

Sessions, in my experience only go one of two ways. They are remarkably smooth and easy. So easy in fact, you want to click your heels and giggle on the way to your car. Why? Because you can't believe you just got paid to have that much fun! The client was gracious and complimentary and they LOVED everything you did. Or the session is stressful and nerve wracking.

Usually if this happens it's because the client is having a hard time expressing what they want and you're having a tough time translating their poor direction. It happens. Rely on your training, go with your gut and be prepared to interpret nonsense. Stay cool and make it clear that you are there to make them happy and deliver a satisfactory performance. Ideally a client will be able to communicate their desired result. Often however, they cannot.

Chapter 4 - Technology

There was a time not so long ago when voiceover people had it easy with regard to audio technology. Audio recording equipment was so expensive & cumbersome that we were not required to know how it worked. All a talent had to do was show up at the studio & talk into a microphone. Voiceover jobs were not common & were especially scarce outside of major cities. Back then, VO talent were primarily actors & actresses living in New York & Los Angeles.

Things have changed; by & large for the better. But it all depends on whether you feel technology is friend or foe. Having an understanding of the software & hardware that create a vessel for your voice is an essential part of your success as a voice artist.

The advent of new technology means that the voiceover industry has easier, faster, more cost-effective methods of recording than ever before. This also means a greater need for VO & likewise, it means more competition.

VO talent now have the ability to record from anywhere in the world & send their audio to anywhere in the world. It's really a very cool thing & in the last ten years has opened a whole new world of possibilities for VO talent. We are no longer isolated or confined by geography. We work from anywhere for clients everywhere; around the globe. We are not driven from our homes & forced to move when our voices inevitably saturate our immediate area, a common occurrence in years past, especially with broadcasters.

In years gone by it was nearly impossible to build a home recording studio without massive amounts of money & space. Now, a few square feet & $1,000 to $3,000 is all it takes to have a decent recording facility in your house.

You may be asking yourself, "Do I really need a studio?" Yes, you do. It is a standard industry expectation that talent have a recording facility. Having 24hr access to your own equipment is the only way to ensure that you get enough time to practice recording and editing. It has been said that it takes 10,000 hours to become proficient at any skill. This is probably true of your current job. New voice actors spend hours, upon hours in their studio practicing: recording, playing back and editing audio. This is the only way to perfect those skills and become not only proficient but competitive in these expected areas.

If you don't have a studio you'll never be able to practice on your own and get the full benefit of coaching and lessons. Nor will you be able to deliver a final product if a client won't pay for outside studio time. However for many people it's hard to understand spending a few thousand dollars on gear not knowing if they will be a success. This is the conundrum all voiceover actors face early on.

It's imperative that you be able to provide your clients with a consistent quality of sound. Finding "your" voice is a big part of this process. Your *signature sound* isn't just about your vocal traits however. It's also about being able to ensure a client that each time they use you, your audio quality, recording settings, volume, pitch, speed, and over-all sound will be the same.

If building your own studio is not in your budget right now, don't panic. You will have time to budget and plan for a studio. This section is essential whether you are ready for the investment of a home studio or not. The information that follows will help you to understand the technology that allows you to deliver a flawless voiceover.

There are many places you can turn to for aid when building a home studio. Your local major music center will be your best resource & can usually help you every step of the way. Most studios can be built in pieces & added to over time. You may also be able to find a company in your area that will come to your home & construct a studio for you. In New York & LA, these companies are readily accessible.

Ultimately, you need access to a studio whether it be your own or someone else's. You can hire a studio when you need one to avoid the expense of building your own. However, you may find that you don't save money with this way. Having to pay for studio time every time you need to record can become very tiresome & inconvenient, but it is an option. Studios charge a voiceover actor anywhere from $40 to $120 per ½ hour of time.

There are many configurations & options when it comes to building a studio. It sometimes seems endless. The recording needs of voiceover actors are pretty basic. We get looked down upon and often shunned by musicians and more technically advanced audio recording folks for how very limited our needs are. Likewise, everyone has a different opinion about what a studio should or shouldn't have. We've compiled a list of basics. This list defines the bare minimum needed for most digital audio recording studios.

A Computer:
All audio recording is done with computers. This is called digital recording & is currently the standard way to record. You may use either a Mac or a PC for your studio. Both platforms offer different options, as well as pros & cons. You'll need to make a decision about which type of computer to buy based on your budget & the other uses the computer will fulfill for your life & business. You should purchase a desktop if your studio is to be on-site and a laptop if you travel frequently and want to record from the road.

You may be able to use the computer you already have. Ideally, you want an up-to-date model, as recording is specialized and uses a lot of computing power.

Your system will need to have lots of storage space (RAM) since audio files & audio recording sessions are so huge. 3 to 4 GB of RAM is the minimum, 8 or more is average. Hard drive sizes don't matter much anymore as external hard drives are so inexpensive. A

250 or 500 GB hard drive is sufficient and if you run out of room you can expand your storage with an external drive.

You'll need an excellent video card & a sound card that is capable of accepting audio not, just playing it back. Most people only use their home computer to output (play) audio; not to input (record) audio. Store bought computers come with very basic sound cards & yours will likely need to be upgraded (this depends on the type of audio interface you purchase – more on this in a moment.) Should you need to upgrade your sound card, you can purchase one at a computer parts stores, online & at most music super stores.

Your computer will also require a variety of external connectors, cords & cables that will allow the computer to be compatible for integration within a studio. You won't know the exact extent of what you'll need until you have selected the other components of your studio.

Audio Recording Software:
You'll also need audio recording software. The software available to you depends on whether you have chosen a Mac or PC. Some software will work for both systems, others only one or the other. ProTools, Adobe Audition, Audacity, SoundForge, SAW, Garage Band & Cakewalk are just a few of the professional choices available to you.

You should choose software based on compatibility & ease of use. Some software require additional hardware to operate properly. Extra hardware components may not mean a better studio but will definitely mean more money.

Most audio recording software all work in the same basic way. They all perform the same functions as the basic needs of audio producers are largely all the same, especially in voiceover. You need not by the most robust (ProTools) or most expensive software (ProTools) because these systems far exceed a voiceover actors needs. In the grand-scheme of audio recording, we only use about 10% of the total capability of most of these programs. Please remember these same systems are used to record, mix and master music, including full orchestral compositions. The needs of voiceover actors are very base by comparison.

You should however take a class in audio recording / editing. Your voiceover coach may offer these classes. Most community colleges offer such classes. If you can't find one pay a local college student, musician or budding audio engineer to teach you privately. Make it clear that you are learning how to record for voiceover and that your primary objective is single track, single channel (mono), recording and editing.

Microphone:
There are many microphones on the market & they all serve different needs. For VO artists, a condenser vocal microphone is recommended. I favor broadcast microphones since they are built for the purpose of speaking not singing. Don't ask a musician, they'll tell you that broadcast
mics stink. But having a broadcasting background, our opinion is simple; 250,000 broadcasters can't be wrong.

The Electro-Voice RE20 & RE27 are excellent mics that are used in radio stations all across the world. They are also moderately priced microphones. This was my mic of choice for over a decade. Other notable and excellent microphones include: Rode NT1 & NT2, The Harlan Hogan Signature microphone, The Neumann TLM 102 & 103, and U87, The Sennheiser 416 shotgun mic and my new favorite for the sound and price, the Sennheiser MK4. But there are many, many others.

When selecting the right mic you want to work with a reputable dealer of audio equipment. Make sure they know that you are seeking a mic for voiceovers, not singing or music recording. That will help them to steer you in the right direction.

Never try to cut costs by using a computer or USB microphone. They are not professional grade & will not meet recording standards. Your microphone must possess an XLR microphone input.

Choose a mic only after having listened to many of them. You want to test different ones and hear yourself on a variety of mics. You also want (whenever possible) recordings of you on different mics so that you can compare sound and quality.

You can do these tests by paying a studio with multiple microphones to allow you to come in and demo them. You can also ask microphone retailers to allow you to do a demo test and if you make friends with other voiceover actors they may allow you to come into their studios to hear yourself on their mics. Offer to take them to lunch, that usually does the trick!

Also some microphone manufacturer (Neumann / Sennheiser in particular) offer test or demo mics that they will ship to your home for you to try before you buy. This way you know you're making the best selection for your voice and your recording space.

An Audio Interface:
An interface is an external device that connects your microphone to your computer. It by-passes your computer's on-board sound drivers & allows for better, cleaner recording. They are small & in some cases portable. The interface you purchase has a lot to do with the type of microphone you buy & the computer you use.

There are an incredible number of interface choices and price points. You'll need a single 9 (one microphone) or dual (two mic) input interface depending on the number of microphones you plan on having. You don't need a complicated or expensive interface. There are many great models for under $300. You'll want to decide between USB, Firewire and Thunderbolt connectivity. Interface technology will require some additional research on your part. I recommend The Voice Actors Guide to Home Recording, an excellent and funny book by Harlan Hogan.

A Compressor, Noise Reducer, or Pre-amp:
Depending on the microphone you choose and the recording pattern or 'direction' of the mic, you may need one of these pieces of equipment to aid in any number of needed enhancements.

Compressors and noise reducers create a more focused sound that aids in the reduction of background noise. A compressor works to focus the mic so that it pinpoints the strongest, most prevalent noise. That noise would be YOU as you stand in front of it & speak. Without a compressor some microphones can sound rather flat or hollow.

Pre-amps add additional gain to the mic and usually brighten the microphones sound. For instance an RE20 or RE27 microphone NEEDS a pre-amp called a Cloud Lifter. Without this little magic box, the mic is somewhat dark and a tad muddy.

Most additional processing (if it's used) is achieved by voiceover actors in post production. This literally means after the recording is complete as opposed to while it's happening. Your recording software should come with some standard, built-in, effects or post-processing options. They pretty much all do. It is typically trial and error to find the right processing to subtly enhance your audio. Subtle is key, clients will usually reject audio that sounds too processed.

You may also find that the items discussed in this section are unnecessary for your studio, and that's a good thing! The best studio is one that offers pure sound that relies on little to no bells and whistles to be professional and usable. Your primary pieces of equipment – computer, microphone, and interface – should be of high enough quality that they need little to no assistance to achieve a great sounding recording.

Speakers:

Also professionally called monitors. You want to get the best you can afford. Speakers are very important because they allow you to accurately play back & hear what you are recording so that you can detect any problems.

Computer speakers will not do. They are not powerful enough to detect the subtle nuances of sound necessary for audio editing. You want professional grade speakers. They don't need to be enormous either. 4 or 6 inch speakers will be more than sufficient. Guitar Center and Sam Ash are excellent sources for monitors.

Essential Incidentals:

You will need a microphone cable to connect your mic to your audio interface & one or more surge protectors for the rest of your equipment. You may want to invest in a U.P.S.; Uninterrupted Power Supply BackUp. You will also need a microphone stand, possibly a shock mount, & a copy board which can simply be a cork board that is in full view & easy reach while you record.

A pop filter is another must have – they are cheap & worth every penny. A pop filter lessens the harsh mouth noises that can pop on-mic, known as "plosives", that most commonly occur when you say a word with a hard P or B on mic; such as "poor" or "boy". There are two varieties; nylon mesh and metal. The metal offers superior plosive reduction, however the nylon version with alter the frequency response of your microphone, which could alter your voice. The experts at Neumann Sennheiser recommend sticking with nylon as a result.

Headphones are needed too. You need a way to hear yourself while you record. They must be professional grade, ear buds will not work for a studio. Good headphones cost $50 to $200 dollars.

Building the Studio:

Now that you have started becoming familiar with all the necessary components of your studio, the next important thing to consider is where to put your studio.

Your studio is technically comprised of two parts - a studio control center & a vocal booth. Your control center is where most of your equipment lives. A desk or table can hold your computer, interface, compressor, speakers, additional hardware, & office necessities.

Your vocal booth needs to be in very close proximity to your desk & equipment. Your microphone, stand & headphones will live in the booth. The two parts of the studio need to be close to one another since the cables that connect your mic to your interface & computer will need to run through the wall or under the door to your booth.

This may sound like it needs to be a large space, but it should be rather small. There are some necessities & money savers to consider while building this environment.

My philosophy is simple: if money is an issue, sacrifice appearance. You cannot skimp on your equipment. It needs to be top notch, but you can save money on the visual appeal of your studio. It doesn't need to be pretty. As long as your spouse permits it – aesthetics be damned! Your recording space can be practical & effective (but ugly).

Walk-in closets & small bedrooms make great studio spaces. As do basements & attics. And any closet can easily be converted into a vocal booth. A small space is best for your booth. Acoustically, you want sound to have the least amount of space to travel.

If you do not have an available closet consider hiring a contractor or handyman who can quickly & cheaply build one for you. Select the right space around an existing wall with an electrical outlet. Then build a three sided frame with a tightly fitted, solid core door. Insulate the hell out of the walls. There's no such thing as too much

129

insulation in the booth because it acts as sound dampening material. Sheetrock the walls & mud the interior & exterior. To save money, you can sand & paint the structure yourself. For slightly more money, you can outfit it with a tightly fitted window so that you don't become claustrophobic in the booth. You can add additional noise reduction by framing a double door – one that opens in and one that opens out. Lighting solutions are easy; use your electrical outlet for a lamp or use battery powered LED fixtures.

Talk to contractors about your needs & budget. I once had a general contractor build me a booth that he lovingly called a "dog house". It was cheaply constructed & not at all attractive. But, it served its purpose & it allowed me to make money. It was small and much like a dog house it was only large enough to walk into, turn around, and walk back out.

If money is not a factor you can purchase a modular booth. They come in kits or fully assembled & can be purchased online. They come "fully loaded" with everything you need to have an instant booth anywhere in your house. They can also be moved should you change locations. Vocals Booths To Go, Studio Bricks and Whisper Room are all great companies.

When you are selecting the room or area of your home for your studio, be aware of your home's plumbing. You don't want your mic to be too close to a source of running water behind walls. Most voice actors have a no flushing rule for their household when they are in the booth, me included.

Likewise, be aware of heating or cooling vents. Your booth can get very hot if you are behind a closed door for long periods of time. But moving, forced air will also be heard on mic. If a vent is already inside a closet you have choose for a booth, you may need to shut down your heat or AC in order to record. I have to do that as well! As do most other voiceover actors.

Also the fewer windows the room or space has the better. Never place a mic too close to a window as windows are very difficult to sound proof without making them look horrible both inside & outside your home.

You're studio will be using a lot of "juice" in a very small space. An isolated or independent circuit breaker is best to prevent surges & interference from other electronics & appliances throughout your home. Sound travels... yes, even through your outlets. A professional electrician can easily assess your needs & let you know what would be involved in isolating the outlets being used for your studio.

Sound proofing is an essential part of any studio. With the exception of modular vocal booths that come pre-proofed, all vocal booths need sound proofing. Professional sound proofing comes in large, dense, heavy foam boards, or slabs that are wrapped in a heavy colored canvas. They are custom fitted to the size of your booth & professionally installed. This option is expensive & can easily cost more than all your equipment combined.

You can also purchase sound proofing sheets from your local music mega store. They come in kits & individual sheets. They are light weight; charcoal colored foam that is either "egg carton" patterned or rippled. They can be cut to suit your space & you can install them with professional adhesive. The most well known brand is Auralex.

There are also many inexpensive ways to sound proof. Carpet padding is an excellent although ugly material. Old blankets, acoustic ceiling tiles, and just about any type of foam can all be wrapped in fabric and adhered to walls with heavy duty adhesive.

The less expensive methods make it essential that you cover as much of the booths exposed wall space as possible, floor to ceiling & wall to wall. Don't forget the inside of the door & make sure you proof around your viewing window if your booth has one. If you have a very high ceiling you may need to drop the ceiling down by using sound proofing to fill some of the space at the top.

Your end result should be a "dead" room. When you clap your hands, make noise, or yell inside your booth, the sound should die quickly with little echo. If you've accomplished this you've done as well as can be expected for a home studio.

Most VO talent- even at the most advanced level don't have a strong audio recording and engineering background. We know and understand how to use the equipment we have and that's about it.

Trouble shooting, studio upgrades, and new technology often require friends, experts, consultants and lots of patience. You don't have to know everything but you do need to have a basic understanding of the science, engineering and electrical demands of a home studio.

In my opinion it's far more important that you become a proficient audio editor. Your client doesn't expect you to masterfully engineer a session all by yourself – they just want a clean, quality recording. They do however expect that you can make preliminary edits to the audio and deliver a mistake free file.

It's imperative that you play and experiment with your chosen audio recording software and become very comfortable with its functions. Consider taking a class at a local community college or watch loads of tutorials on You Tube. You'll get the hang of it.

Recording Settings & Mic Techniques

There are a few industry standards when it comes to how your voice should be recorded. If you have recording knowledge, this section will make a good deal of sense. If not, your goal is to explore these concepts further. You will need to understand these settings in order to best use the audio recording software you purchase.

▶ Audio should be recorded at a sample rate of 44100 or 48000 MHZ with 16 bit resolution unless you are told to do otherwise by a client. Mono recording for dry voice is preferred since the human voice is mono and the files take up less space. We hear in stereo but we emit in mono so a stereo is just an unnecessarily large file.

Editing takes a long time to master. Take it slowly & carefully in the beginning. Voiceover talent are NOT required or expected to fully produce their audio with music & sound effects, so your job is to be able to perform basic editing function that 'clean' the audio in the first round of post production.

Basic edits include deleting mistakes, gaps & unnecessary audio from a recording. You may also choose to edit your breaths out of your auditions. It is always best to err on the side of caution when editing. Gaps & space can be further tightened by the client, so keep things loose. However if the edits you create are too tight & don't leave enough space, you may damage the file thus making it unusable. You'll have to rerecord everything. This will cost the client time and money. Most beginners become edit happy and are prone to creating excessively tight edits. Space is good. Your edits should mimic the natural pauses created during speech. If your files sound choppy and fast you are likely editing too much.

Microphone anxiety is another common problem for beginners. The only way to avoid it is to spend lots of time behind a mic. The more time you spend on mic, practicing, playing, & goofing around, the more comfortable the process will be. Also, the more you will understand what you can & cannot do behind a mic.

All microphones have specific settings and quirks that will enhance or decrease the quality of a recording. *But* a mic alone does nothing. It's all up to you, the person using it, to make it work the way you want it to. The mic cannot manipulate the sound of your voice without your assistance & participation in the process.

The material to follow will help you get familiar with microphones; hopefully you have one to practice with. If not, now would be a good time to consider the investment or you can start booking time at a local studio to practice.

▶ Stand or sit in an upright position. Try not to slouch or restrain your abdomen when recording but remain relaxed. If you take a stiff or unnatural posture when recording you're VO will sound stiff.

▶ Stay about 3 to 5 inches from the microphone. Usually a palm's length away or a full hand length.

▶ Speak in a normal or louder than normal speaking tone, never softer. If you tend to be soft spoken then you really need to speak up. If a read requires that you must whisper, move a little closer to the mic. If a read requires you to yell, back away from the mic. Try to maintain a constant volume. Your headphones will help you to maintain proper volume.

▶ Be conscious & aware that every movement you make could be picked up by the mic & end up on the recording. If you tap, bump or disrupt the mic you must stop & begin again. Try not to rustle papers either.

▶ Refrain from cursing & general use of vulgarity while behind the mic; often times talent get into the habit of cursing when they goof – don't make this mistake. If you forget to edit your profanity you may send the client a file that includes an expletive they did not bargain for.

▶ Isolate your breathing so that breaths & words don't run together. This means that every time you need to breathe while on mic you must pause before you breathe, take the breath, pause again, & then begin speaking again. They don't need to be long pauses; just enough to leave room for the breath to be removed from the audio file later.

▶ Make sure to soften hard consonant sounds that will "pop" on mic. Words that have hard P's or B's such as POOR or BOY should be said with a soft emphasis so that your lips don't create a pop when they are spoken. Popping can be difficult to control. Pops ruin a recording & make them completely useless for the folks who hired you to record in the first place. You must be aware of when you pop so that you can correct the mistake. Put your hand to your face palm forward and say 'boy'. Did you feel air hitting your palm? That rush of air is what causes the plosive. Say the word again and soften the B until little to no air comes in contact with your hand.

▶ Be careful of over pronounced S words, such as SINISTER. If you don't soften the S sounds it will sound very sibilant & unpleasant. Sometimes microphones can be the cause of sibilance. You may have to adjust the angle of the mic to reduce over-pronounced S sounds.

▶ Mouth Noise is another very important thing to avoid. When your mouth is dry your tongue, gums, & lips can "stick" making soft smacking sounds. Make sure you have plenty of water during a session & be sure to open your mouth wide when speaking. Green apples, lemons, olive oil, & other acidic or lubricating foods can lessen or eliminate mouth noise. I keep my fridge stocked with Motts Green Apple apple sauce for just this purpose. The older we get the worse mouth noise becomes and some people are just more prone to it than others. Like anything else on mic, awareness is the key to taking preventive and preemptive measures.

Directed Sessions

Clients often request directed recording sessions from their talent. They may ask for a directed audition or to be able to direct a paid job. Traditionally, a directed session is done in person but technology allows us to utilize other methods so a client can have control of the audio they are receiving & you are voicing.

ISDN is the best way to have a directed session (see more about ISDN in the section titled Audio Delivery Methods).

Phone patch is also very good for directed sessions. Phone patch technology is something you may want to add to your studio. Phone patch equipment allows you to talk to a client by essentially converting your microphone & headphones into a telephone.

The client hears you through your mic, & you hear them through your headphones. You are responsible for recording the session but they have the ability to direct the session & tell you exactly how to read & record the copy.

Traditional phone patch equipment is an added expense; instead outfit a speaker phone into your booth. You can use an adapter to split your phone line & run the second line into the booth. Purchase a speaker phone & keep it wall mounted near the microphone.

Make sure it's close so that a client can hear you loud & clear while you are recording. This gives you hands free communication & offers your clients the directing ability they will undoubtedly need.

Just about every cell phones has speaker phone capabilities, it may work well in your booth for directed sessions too. Using your phone (cordless or cell) with headphones avoid the possibility of the client being recorded as well. Whatever method you choose make certain to test your phone patch system before having an actual call with a client.

Audio Delivery Methods

It is only crucial that you understand what these things are, not that you have access to all of them, all at once. These items are important because people in this industry talk about them & use them often.

Wave: A .wav file (wave file) is raw & pure audio. When something is recorded into a computer the audio recording software creates a session file first and then defaults to .wav for rendering purposes. (It's called this because the visual pattern that recorded sound creates is a series of peaks & valleys that look like something a surfer would love to conquer.)

Wave files are very large & require a good amount of storage space since they take up lots of room in e-mail. They are measured in megabytes or MB. The average :60 second radio commercial is about 6MB once edited. But waves are the purest & highest quality available even though their size can sometimes make them inconvenient. Most email programs restrict the sending or receiving of anything larger than 10MB. Anything over 20MB will take a very, very long time to send and to receive via email. It's just takes too long to upload or download the files for email to be a practical way to send .wav files.

When you travel to a recording studio, it is likely .wav files that will be used to create the final audio production. Clients will often request that you ship them audio in .wav format, too. Since .wav is simply too large to send via a standard email attachment (unless it's a very, very short recording) you would upload the file with FTP technology, a free-ware website like WeTransfer.com, or A Drop Box or Sound Cloud account. We Transfer is free and easy to use and will work for most standard recordings.

MP3: Mp3 is a compressed form of .wav. It's a process that allows a .wav to be shrunk for easier transport. The quality is not as high as a .wav but Mp3 is a standard way to send & receive audio. That is because it is small, universal & any degeneration of the audio is usually undetectable providing that you create the Mp3 at a high rate of compression (128K for mono / 256K for stereo).

A 60 second commercial in mp3 format is 2MB or smaller. This makes it easy to send mp3s via email.

You will often hear Mp3 referred to as a lossy format. That's because there is a loss of data when the Mp3 is created. Audio purists and high-end clients do not accept Mp3 as a way to receive voiceover files.

ISDN: ISDN is a digital phone line; a dedicated connection that acts like the internet. In conjunction with some rather pricy equipment (a Zephyr) an ISDN line is linked directly to your studio.

Two parties that have ISDN can "dial in" to one another. A voice artist can perform as though they are live in someone's studio. The receiving studio records the session onto their equipment. The talent never actually records anything & there is no additional delivery of material. Once the call is ended the client has what they need. The quality is exceptional but this technology is dying out.

ISDN lines are not cheap – having & maintaining one of these lines can cost a few hundred to a thousand dollars a month depending on usage. This type of investment is usually made by professionals with many years vested in the industry, & those that have a steady stream of day-to-day work that requires ISDN. For the time being, find a local recording studio that offers ISDN should one of your clients request it.

Make sure you find out the types of fees you will incur at the studio; this way you can let a client know upfront how much it costs & that they will have to pay the extra costs. ISDN lines are rapidly becoming a thing of the past as new and more affordable options that are internet based become available.

FTP: FTP is a way to upload & download large audio & video files via the use of an Internet server. Companies & voiceover artists that deal with lots & lots of audio find this to be a convenient way to send & receive audio in large amounts.

Instead of sending an mp3 or a .wav via email, a VO talent can record audio & then upload the files (using FTP software) to a secure FTP server. The person receiving the audio can then retrieve & download it.

"File Transfer Protocol" can be used to send information safely over the internet. You can send files to someone else's FTP without having one yourself. FTP software is very inexpensive. Having your own FTP will cost more but may be a worthwhile investment for you in the near future.

AIFF: "Audio Interchange File Format". A high quality, uncompressed form of audio that is very similar to a .wav. It was originally created & received on Macintosh computer systems, but has now become a standard with PC users also. Unlike Mp3 it is a "lossless" audio file.

SOURCE CONNECT: A relatively new technology created by a company called Source Elements, it offers codec based, studio to studio (computer to computer) recording capability. Source Connect is a relatively standard tool in the industry now and continues to offer inventive solutions that are meant to replace ISDN.

IPDTL / InQuality / Source Connect Now: lots of names but they all do the same thing! This is the newest technology in the race to replace ISDN. It is internet based, browser based, bi-direction streaming. This means that you can connect two studios & record from either end & achieve broadcast quality sound via the internet. It is new, & at times unreliable. However, the industry largely seems to agree that this technology is the future of voiceover recording and that it will be the new standard in terms of how voiceover actors and studios connect.

The internet & email will likely be the technologies you use the most often for your voiceover business. If you still do not know how to use the Internet or email, now would be a good time to start learning those skills. I'm still amazed by the amount of web illiteracy that exits. To conduct any sort of business today you must have a better than basic understanding of how to use the internet. The following section is a guideline of etiquette for doing business over the web.

The average email without an attachment is usually 33KB (kilobyte) in size, which is very small. The average email account is able to receive lots of files but is not capable of sending or receiving large emails that include attachments of 10MB or bigger. (It takes 1,000 KB of information to make 1 MB).

Most "free" email accounts like Hotmail, MSN, Yahoo, Gmail, etc. don't allow you to send large files, there is a maximum or a limit to what you can send and receive. So you may have to contact some paid providers about setting up an account that is your own that have few if any restrictions.

The maximum number of MBs I can send to in email is 22. But just because I can send it doesn't mean you can receive it! Only send really large files if they have been requested or if you have received permission to send them.

Nothing is more bothersome then the fledgling talent that sends a 16MB demo. It's rude & presumptuous. Don't risk upsetting a client by unknowingly maxing out their email in-box, or clogging the pipeline.

The number of mega bytes or MBs a recipient can receive will vary depending on the email provider they use. But you don't want to waste time asking every person how large an email attachment they can receive. So, keep it simple & keep everything at 3MBs or less. That is usually a safe zone.

It also helps for forwarding purposes because you never know who might forward your demo on to another party or how large a file that person can accept.

If you are sending your demo out in an email to a prospective client always use Mp3; nothing else. Stay away from "Real Player" files, "Windows Media Player" files, AIFF or any other form of audio that requires a specific type of software or computer system to create, "read" and play the data. Mp3 is universal (however, mp4 is not).

Mac users need to be especially careful in this regard. You don't want people to "work" to hear your demo. You also don't want to give them the impression that you don't know the proper way to send basic audio.

Λ major pct peeve of those who receive voice demos & auditions is talent who don't properly label their mp3 files. Don't just name the mp3 of your demo "Commercial Demo". Do you have any idea how many people do that? No one can properly ID one demo from the next when 25,000 talent all have a file labeled "Commercial Demo."

The proper & courteous thing to do is label your mp3 in the following manner: "Sally Smith demo 2007.mp3". Make sure that the subject line is also easy to identify: "Subject: VO Artist For Hire".

Keep the body of your emails short & sweet. Don't write a novel, a full bio, or loads of info about recent work.

Be courteous & to the point. Nothing you write will matter more than the demo attached to the email. Be sure to include contact info & of course include a link to your website should you have one. Create a standard email "signature" that appears at the bottom of all your emails and that will automatically generate every time you create a new email.

When sending a mass email, send it blind or as a blind carbon copy - BCC.

If you have a list of 100 ad agencies & you are going to send your demo to all of them via one email, BCC ensures that no one can read anyone else's email address. Otherwise you've basically broadcasted everyone's email address to 100 other people. It's the electronic equivalent of handing out someone's phone number without getting their permission.

Lastly, don't ask for permission to send a demo. Anything that makes a recipient work harder to receive your material will not work to your advantage. Should you follow the rules provided in this section and pay close attention to the size of the file your are sending – remember 3MB or less – you have no reason to ask for permission prior to sending.

Hiring a Studio

If you choose to hire a studio, you need to carefully review the audio recording requirements in this booklet so that you can discuss your needs when you interview studios.

The studio you select should be easily accessible & should offer quality audio services at a fair price to you. When selecting a studio you also want to find one that specializes in audio for advertising. **A studio for musicians will probably not employ people that will be of much help to you in voiceovers. They are capable of recording you, but they may not be able to offer helpful criticism or advice.**

Depending on where you are in the country studio time will range from $75.00 to $400.00 per hour. Many studios add extra fees for things like an mp3 conversion, a master copy of the session or for a phone patch. Try to avoid places with these add-on fees.

Also make sure that the studio you choose will allow you to schedule bump times. If your client estimates that a session will take an hour you should book a one hour session with a ½ hour bump. The bump ensures that you don't pay for the extra studio time if you don't need it.

Lastly, ask the studio if they will offer you 15 minute & ½ hour rates. Most studios have a minimum booking time of one hour, but you may be able to convince them of a reduced time slot & fees for things like auditions if they know you will be using them often & recommending them to others. It never hurts to ask.

The technology used in audio changes often. A voiceover artist must be proactive with new equipment, new mediums & new styles of recording.

Young people take to new technology very quickly but the older we get the more frightened we become of change. Don't let this happen to you. Over the years we've seen two types of talent: those who innovate & those who die (figuratively speaking). Many careers die off because of a lack of proficient in new technology. Always stay current!

Voice talent, author, and coach Harlan Hogan has written an excellent book on the subject of home and mobile recording for voiceover talent.

I highly recommend purchasing <u>The Voice Actors Guide to Home Recording</u> to further your recording knowledge. It can be purchased online at VoiceoverEssentials.com.

Chapter 5 – Creating Demos

A demo is the single most important item in your audio arsenal. It is the ultimate marketing tool for voiceover talent. For most talent, it's also a nerve-wracking, nail-biting process that only becomes more difficult as your career blooms. But it doesn't have to be.

The demo you create is all prospective clients will know of you. Demo(s) help you define your niche and areas of expertise. So it must be the best it can be & you should be very proud of it. This is your chance to shine & show off your skills.

I do not recommend that you start the process of creating a demo until you have trained extensively with one or more coaches. You should feel confident that you know all there is to know about beginning a VO career before proceeding with this all-important process. The demo should be strategized for marketability before it is built.

It's important that every VO talent 'find their voice' before even thinking about creating a demo. Finding your sound & having a unique approach takes lots of practice & time. For many talent, it also requires coaching & vocal training. Training is the number one way in which talent find their 'signature' or niche sound.

You cannot rush the process of demo creation. Too many talent are in a hurry & want to get their demos done fast. Acting is one of the few professions where folks want to rush the learning process & jump right into making money. But how can you expect to make money & be successful if you haven't allowed yourself adequate time to train? If you've never run a day in your life, you wouldn't try to run a 5k marathon without conditioning your body first.

Most professional jobs require years of training & a hefty educational investment. No, you won't pay as much for your education as a doctor or an attorney, but that's because both of those professions require 6-12 years of schooling. Your voice endeavor may require 2-4 years of training, coaching, practice & learning before you are even ready to make a demo & present your voice to potential clients. Take your time & don't feel pressured. You want to do this right...right?

A demo should be no more than one minute. That's right; you have 60 seconds in which to showcase your work. Here's the scary part – most people don't even listen that long. In most cases the name of the game is "you suck" & you have five seconds or less in which to impress the listener. If they're not impressed, your demo is in the trash – gone in 60 seconds, so to speak.

Another reason having a brief demo is important is the advent of MP3, electronic audio & email correspondence. You will frequently send your demo via email. Audio files are big & take up lots of room in an email. It's a simple courtesy to keep things small for that reason.

Don't bury your best piece or try to build anticipation with a demo. Always put your best work first. There are so many mediocre demos in circulation that people literally start with the notion that you're bad & you have to prove them of otherwise & fast.

Don't mix & match various industries and types of VO on one demo. Each type of demo you wish to create should stand alone. Like stays with like; gone are the days of the five-minute demo that is a massive compilation of everything you've ever done or everything you're confident you can do.

You must create a niche for yourself & make sure that your demo showcases your strong points. Not every VO person is good at everything, nor are they all extremely diverse. You should focus on what makes you unique so that you always stand out & are able to make a name for yourself, striving to get work in one particular area of the industry.

The terms "demo tape" or "reel" are things of the past. Any form of tape, be it cassette or otherwise is no longer an acceptable means of broadcast quality audio, & it hasn't been for some time. Good luck finding a potential source of work that even owns a cassette player in which to listen to one. Cassettes are a dinosaur. The original term reel comes from the days when audio was recorded on analog tape. A reel to reel machine was used to record and copy dubs of voiceover demos. So back then you didn't have a demo CD or mp3; you had a demo reel.

Don't try to skip steps & cut corners when creating your demo. The competition is fierce & plentiful. There are some stellar demos out there. Yours must be on par with others in your experience level. Do not skimp on the production aspect of your demo. A "dry" demo - , one without music or sound-effects is not a demo…it's just a sample & it won't get you professional work, nor will it help to further your career. Likewise, one fully produced, 60 second commercial is not enough either. It shows no range or versatility & leaves people thinking – "that's all you've got?"

Do not use your demo as a sounding board or pitch. Many new talent recite a small message at the beginning of their demo saying things like "Hi, I'm Gary Boy & this is my VO demo. If you like what you hear you can reach me at…" This is a huge mistake. It's unprofessional & completely unnecessary. If your demo is properly labeled & named then you've covered all that.

The production of your demo or demos must be 60 seconds of perfection. There is nothing worse than a great voice that's been buried behind bad edits, terrible music beds & horrible sound effects. So you have two choices; if you are skilled in the ways of producing, editing & general audio recording you can produce for yourself. Or you can hire someone to do it for you.

If you take the latter route make sure that you find a professional that understands & works with voiceovers on a regular basis. Just because your cousin Larry owns a music studio where musicians record, doesn't mean he knows diddly about voiceovers.

Listen to examples of a potential producer's work & always get a satisfaction guarantee in writing. You want assurance that if the final product is not to your liking, you don't have to pay for it or that they will continue working until it is to your liking. The studio should be willing to agree that they will work with you to create a product you're happy with.

Don't expect it to be cheap. A professional quality demo can range in price from $800 to $4000 or more. Do lots of homework before starting the process. Remember this will be your most widely used marketing tool. Without it you have no hope of getting a voice job & the studios that create demos know it.

Buyers beware! When it comes to audio production you get what you pay for. If someone offers to record your demo for $50; sure it's cheap but will it be a good demo? Probably not. Don't make the mistake of hiring a producer who is a beginner & has no more production experience than you have with VO.

Whenever you are auditioning a studio ask to hear no less than 5 demos they have produced. If any of the demos sound alike or if you hear the same script or music repeated DO NOT employ that studio. Chances are they are cookie cutter, assembly line style producers.

Your demo should be customized to you. It should be singular to you. There are a lot of expensive, shady companies that make demos from a production template. This is bad news for you & any other talent that has used them.

Make sure that the studio you have in mind offers the latest equipment, guidance & the means by which to deliver your demo in multiple forms. The studio should act as more than just a place to record. During the recording session they should direct and coach you to ensure the best possible performances. Again, you must make certain this is something they have done before with proven success.

It is also worthwhile to note that many top VO talent – those who also possess plenty of production skills - choose not to produce their own demo. Sometimes talent are just a little too close to their work & it takes another trained ear to determine what will market your voice in the best light. It's the same reason why authors have editors. You are bringing in an impartial person to check for mistakes & evaluate the effectiveness of the demo. So, very rarely do I recommend that VO artists create their own demos.

If you are a moderately experienced talent already & you are trying to save money you can create a catalog of some of your existing work. Bring those pieces to a skilled producer. They can edit a demo together by picking & choosing the best pieces from the audio you already have. However this is a band-aid method as this offers little control of the marketability and presentation of the demo. Usually work you have actually done is not demo worthy. The demo selection process is picky and painstaking.

Next, we'll outline the most lucrative types of voiceovers & their corresponding demos. Each one of these demo types is used to market your voice to a specific industry that uses VO. You should become familiar with all of them. Many voice artists have multiple demos to highlight their abilities in these areas. Don't feel obligated to have a demo for each industry; however a few is advisable. Understanding these voiceovers, their purpose and how to properly present demos in each of these genres is key.

Commercial: A commercial demo is made up of radio & TV spots for a variety of different retail & non-retail businesses. It should features your ability to "sell" on a commercial level.

Your commercial demo is your primary demo because it is both universal and (if created correctly) will feature a solid, clear presentation of your core or signature sound. As a result, clients will often turn your commercial demo to get a feel for your abilities before listening to any of your other demos.

Likewise if you do not offer a demo in a particular area (let's say TV Promo), a client will likely listen to your commercial demo as it should give a good indication of your overall skill level and sound.

Commercial demos are relatively narrow demos. 45-60 seconds in length they should show subtle variation or facets of your vocal personality. Use only national, brand-name copy. Also, modern commercial demos are very testimonial heavy as clients want to hear your ability to be real and conversation.

Narration: Everything from audio books to audio used for a stage performance is a narration. Anytime you are telling a story for non-broadcast purposes, it's a narration piece. Reading a story, children's book, or narrating a chain of events are all narrative reads. Examples of well known narration styles are "Moby Dick", "Winnie the Pooh", "Desperate Housewives", "How I Met Your Mother", & "Meerkat Manor."

A narrator can be a first person speaker - someone directly involved in the story they are telling. A first person narrator may be recalling or sharing events from the past or present. Since a first person narrator has a vested interest in the story, their presentation is usually personal and at times emotional since the events taking place directly affect them or someone they know.

A third person narrator is usually impartial. Their job is not to judge or share an opinion but rather to relay events as they unfold. Third person narrators are cool, calm and sometimes icy in their presentation.

Turn to TV networks like Discovery Channel and History Channel to hear great examples of narration work. I'm also a big fan of Animal Planet because almost all of their programming requires some amount of voiceover narration since the animals can't tell their own story! Reality TV as a whole (be it shows about history, science, the future, or nature) has increased narration work by almost double in the last 15 years. Someone has to speak when the subject matter doesn't; it might as well be you!

A narration demo requires that you show off your ability to captivate an audience and hold their attention while telling stories. Once again use national, name-brand copy. Your demo length can be up to one-minute and thirty-seconds since part of what a narration demo helps you to do is display your ability to sustain a long read and keep an audience interested in your for long periods of time.

A standard narration demo will mostly include narrations for TV and film and other entertainment programming. Although audio books are a form of narration, it is best to keep audio book reads on a separate demo just for audio book buyers.

Before venturing into narration and certainly before creating a demo, you need to consider the time commitment that many narration jobs require. Are you able to meet the needs of these buyers?

Many narration jobs are short and sweet. Under an hour in total time, however long-form narrations and audio books can require hundreds of hours of work. You must consider your time not only on-mic recording, but also the time it takes to edit and prepare these jobs for final delivery. Every hour or raw recording takes 2 or 3 hours to edit and prep.

Character: Character work is a very tough arena. Lots of people are capable of average or slightly above-average impressions & impersonations but only the absolute best make money in this area. If you choose to do impressions they must be flawless. But you may find that there is not much demand for them.

On the other hand, humorous pieces are always well received. If you have a good sense of comedic timing & can handle humorous copy, include it in a character demo. If you have a unique character voice that is all your own, feel free to let it shine on this demo.

If you do a fantastic and - most importantly - authentic, foreign dialect, find copy that fits & use that as well. Accents are a difficult arena and many folks make the mistake of thinking they know an accent. If you've never been to the country it's from and you don't have intimate knowledge of the accent, it's best not to attempt it.

Character demos are typically fast paced and the goal is to show off as much vocal gymnastics as you can in 60 seconds. Each character voice you choose for the demo may only speak a few words or a sentence before you move on to the next character.

Sound design is especially important in a character demo because the sound effects, music and vocal effects used in the demo must accentuate the character presentation and lend to the believability of the character.

Do not try to create a skit or a 'play' with your character demo. We find it hokie not entertaining. The characters should be stand-alone and in no way dependant on the voice that comes before or after.

You can transcribe copy from the TV or internet by finding little known or obscure cartoons. Those are usually the best ones to use because it's unlikely anyone will detect that you weren't the 'real' voice.

Video games demos are similar to character demos and follow the same guidelines. They are more physical and vocally, they sound more like you then the rest of your character work.

Sound design is especially important in a character demo because the sound effects, music, and vocal effects used in the demo must accentuate the character presentation and lend to a believability of the character.

TV Promo: Don't mistake this for a commercial demo. A commercial is a commercial whether it's used for radio or TV. A TV promo demo consists of promo work recorded for local & national TV networks, station affiliates, & news dailies. This demo also includes cable TV promo work either local or national.

"And now HBO presents Game of Thrones", "Tonight on the Food Network", "Tomorrow on Dancing with the Stars, don't miss…" are all examples of cable TV promo VO.

News dailies are short promotional pieces that advertise the upcoming events on that day's news program. This work is similar to radio imaging – discussed in detail in the next few pages. A TV promo promotes the TV station itself, not another product or advertiser. Ultimately it promotes the watching of more television.

There are seven major types of TV programming: Comedy, Drama, News, Talk, Movie, Special Interest and Kids Programming. Every show on TV falls into one of these major categories. Even reality TV is branded as either comedy or drama.

There are two types of TV promo demos. The first is called a Network Demo. A Network Demo showcases your ability to be the voice of a major network such a FOX, CBS, ABC, ESPN, MTV, etc. Your job is to prove to network clients that you have a sound or style that is well suited for the overall message and the programming the network offers.

Your network demo would consist of a variety of similar style networks or shows in order to best demonstrate your ability to fit the lifestyle of the network and the viewing audiences and perhaps even a specific type of programming. As a network promo voice you should exemplify the over-all *feel* and message of the network. Remember that networks frequently hire more than one voice. A network may have as many as five regular voices with each voice being utilized to promote a specific type of program.

The second possibility is called an Affiliate TV Promo Demo. TV stations affiliates are the local market "babies" of a parent TV network. CBS is a national network that creates programming and content that airs nationwide on all CBS affiliates. Every major city in the USA has a CBS affiliate station.

Programming on each CBS affiliate throughout the country will vary slightly. Also the station has an obligation to create local content that is pertinent to the wants, needs, and concerns of the viewing area. An example of this is a station's nightly news programming.

Affiliate voices must wear more than one hat. Affiliate stations have far less money than networks and can typically only hire one or two promo voices. Therefore a TV Affiliate Promo Demo must showcase skills that match or fit all of the major programming types. You must present pieces on your demo that display you as a comedy, drama, movie, news and children's programming voice.

These demos should be no more than 70 seconds in length. It is absolutely critical that a TV Promo demo, regardless of which type, is produced with drop-ins and audio segments from TV shows and news broadcasts. The scripts should be real TV Promo copy that you transcribe from TV or the internet.

TV Promo clients are sticklers for authenticity and knowledge of programming. So it is best to have a TV Promo expert producer involved in the creation of your demo.

Radio Imaging: Imaging is all the pre-recorded "stuff" you hear between songs on the radio. (This has nothing to do with the DJ.) Radio station formats vary widely, from rock to hip hop to jazz to female friendly lite rock to country to alternative. What you listen to determines the type of imaging you've been exposed to. Imaging is how a radio station "brands" their position in the marketplace & reiterates their overall message to the listener. (And you thought it was just about playing music.)

There's a lot of money to be made in TV Promo & radio imaging. As a result this type of work is coveted. As a station's "voice" you are an important part of the message they deliver. Since this is an important process to them you can expect to be hired on a contract basis. Stations usually hire their voice for a minimum of one year. So you are guaranteed a monthly fee for 12 months. You provide the voiceover for a combination of small scripts called liners, sweepers & promos that all "sell" the station.

Much like radio formats, the way to deliver imaging reads varies widely. To get an idea of how broad these different reads are, make it a point to listen to a few different stations over the next few weeks & try to identify their primary imaging voice (stations will often have a primary & a few secondary voices) & the style in which they are delivering the read.

An imaging demo consists of a montage of imaging reads. Many talents choose to break these down into format specific demos that showcase their talent & flair for voicing different stations within a particular format. In the beginning you should choose a format that you're well suited for or one that is appealing to you.

Not only is there a knack to recording imaging VO, there is also an art form to the production of imaging. In order to successfully create this type of demo with no prior imaging experience you'll need the talent of a producer that specializes in radio imaging.

A radio imaging demo is the only time that you can break all the rules of sound effects & vocal effects that are usually a big no-no in demos. Anything goes in imaging & the producers have a blast making this audio come to life. You don't want the effects to take away from or over-power your voice. Instead you want them to enhance the demo by giving stations something they are accustomed to hearing.

Movie Trailers: Movie trailer voiceovers are used in TV commercials that advertise a new blockbuster movie, they are also played in the movie theater during previews and they are part of the previews of DVDs. Basically the theater & DVD use is just a longer version.

Movie trailers are not for beginners for one main reason - money. Major motion picture studios & production companies spend millions of dollars making movies in the hopes of earning millions more when they're released. Therefore, these companies spend tens of thousands of dollars on the voiceover that will air in conjunction with the movie's TV "teaser". Not only do beginners not receive work like this, seasoned professionals find it hard to obtain trailer work.

To put this all into perspective, there are only about 50 people in the whole U.S. that record voiceovers for movie trailers. Of those 50, five are heard pretty much every day. Tom Kane, Hal Douglas, Ashton Smith & Howard Parker are just a few of these movie trailer VO guys. They are superstars in the industry & a pleasure to work with.

When was the last time you heard the coming attractions for a movie & the VO was a woman? Ladies, we don't want to burst any bubbles but movie trailer work is dominated by men. Rarely are women heard in an actual movie theatre & not for action/drama films. Women are mainly used for "made for TV" movies on networks like Lifetime & Oxygen so focus on "chick-flicks" if you want to make this sort of demo.

Creating a trailer demo is no different from any other. Find some great copy & work to incorporate many types of reads to display how your voice would sound with different types of movies. Drama, action & comedy are the must-haves. You will need to include clips or sound bites from the movie in order to make a truly authentic trailer demo.

When it comes to trailers your voice quality must be superb. It's often said that movie trailer voices are akin to "the voice of God" because they are that huge, that bright, & that incredible. The entire industry bows down to successful movie trailer voice actors. But remember, they have survived a long road of very hard work to get there.

A prerequisite of this demo would be extensive training with Marice Tobias. She is a high-end voiceover coach known as the 'voice whisperer'. Almost all successful trailer voices have coached with her.

Industrials: Industrials are one of the fastest changing types of voiceovers because their definition is always changing. They are largely teaching tools and there are loads of small sub-genres, including: telephony, e-learning, pharmaceutical and medical narration, text to speech or TTS applications, talking toys, GPS Systems and more.

Here are the basics: They are never broadcast on TV or radio. They are most often used for educational & instructional purposes, which can range from audio for a college class or online course, a company's sales & training video, tutorials for consumers, or a home-use "do it yourself" CD-ROM. These types of jobs don't typically pay very well. Industrial success comes from volume work.

Industrials are the least creative of all voiceover jobs, however technical accuracy and studio quality are paramount. Strong editing skills are necessary too. Since this area of VO is so conservative and corporate, many of the speech quirks that make actors interesting or unique are frowned upon in this area.

When negotiating the terms of an industrial job, get all the facts first & find out exactly what the job entails so that you can get the most money upfront or so that you can create a restricted use contract.

Always try to get the script in advance too, because industrials often include very difficult words, strange terms & proper names that you will be expected to pronounce properly. Pharmaceutical & medical VOs are enough to make the average voice artist's skin crawl.

Pronunciation sources include: the client, doctors, pharmacists, universities, foreign consulates, dictionaries, etc. Ask; "How would you read this?" And always be prepared to see this: "The new diagnostic analysis system devised by Dr. Zixery Sighillen is as simple as his name".

The delivery of industrial material should always be presented in a way that appropriately matches the client, company, or theme of the script. You are looking to be friendly on a professional level. You are selling a product. You are teaching someone how to do something. These reads are the most laid-back & matter of fact. Industrial demos are usually short & don't show a lot of range or diversity.

If you wish to make an industrial demo & don't have any industrial material to work with, talk to your doctor, dentist, vet, travel agent, or a charity group – you will undoubtedly be able to find some pamphlets or info that you can turn into a usable industrial script. Reading the instructions that come with a child's "assembly required" toy is another script option.

Telephony: On-Hold-Messages, Phone Prompts, IVR:
On-hold-messages are fast, easy, widely available work that typically doesn't pay well. But beginners will find much success with on-hold-message companies if they market themselves properly.

A message-on-hold is no different than any other type of VO really. You are choosing a style of read & presenting it in a friendly, familiar, & pleasing manner. You are acting as a representative of a particular company & you are informing your audience of things they may not have known, such as hours of operation, directions, maybe even this month's "special". You are still voicing for advertising purposes, but it's a softer, more laid back feel. A message-on-hold demo should follow all the standard demo rules & you should always use national or regional copy, never local.

Since most messages-on-hold are made up of long scripts that incorporate :15 to :30 voice segments make sure you are providing FULL messages. Don't chop a message or montage it as you would a commercial demo. You may only fit between two or three examples on the demo but that is okay.

Phone Prompts and I.V.R (Interactive Voice Response) are common forms of telephony VO. "Press one for_____, Press two for _____." We've all heard these. Your VO needs to be extremely professional, clear & devoid of almost all emotion. You just want to sound friendly, but sounding like a human is sometimes optional in prompts. Some companies actually prefer that you come across sounding a bit robotic, while others want a very natural & friendly delivery.

The voiceover community does not give MOH & IVR enough credit. They may not be terribly glamorous jobs, but think about how cool it would be to be the "phone" voice of a major retailer, airline, cell phone company, utility provider; etc. It's actually a great credibility booster & experience that you can usually get in large quantities (even when you're very new); even though it's one of the most loathed forms of advertising by the consumer.

IVR and prompts are an important part of a company's brand image too. Large companies like banks and utility providers that have a high call volume will contract their IVR voice on a monthly or yearly basis because they update their system so frequently. Unlike message-on-hold, IVR and prompt work can be very time consuming. A single job may contain thousands of individual prompts that range in size from a word or two to whole sentences.

IVR & prompt demos should showcase a pleasant neutral use of your voice with a slowly paced delivery. Your focus should be on your diction and the clarity of your voice. Music and sound effects are not advisable since IVR and prompt jobs do not utilize either. You may also create a demo that presents on-hold, IVR and phone prompt pieces all together.

Foreign language: If you're bilingual you should feature separate demos for the other languages you speak proficiently. You must be fully fluent & literate in these languages. Most clients demand authenticity when they seek a foreign speaker; therefore, it is only recommended that you create this type of demo if you are originally from another country. Authenticity is a must when it comes to language. So if you hail from France, you should make a demo in French, not English. Unless you have the ability to completely, 100% mask or hide your accent.

Should you choose to create a foreign language demo, you would simply select the type of demo you wish to create (commercial, narration, etc) and create a demo based on the guidelines we present in this book. The only difference is that the copy you select will be in the language you plan to present.

The demo you create is all prospective clients will know of you. Demo(s) help you define your niche and areas of expertise. So it must be the best it can be & you should be very proud of it. This is your chance to shine & show off your skills.

Demo Scripts

Once you have selected the type of demo(s) you wish to create, the next step is copy selection. Great copy is like a weapon – an advertiser takes aim at the target demographic & shoots, firing a message at them. **Choose copy wisely when preparing to make a demo.**

Don't write the copy yourself. Copywriters are the brains behind great advertising campaigns. Nothing is more loathed by the audio & advertising community than bad copy & bad copy is everywhere.

It doesn't matter how great a voice you have, bad scripts can ruin a great demo.
You can find quality copy by transcribing what you hear on the radio or TV & by using text from websites. Be careful of anything too familiar or a VO associated with a celebrity. The listener should believe that the work on your demo is work that you were hired to perform or *could* have been hired to perform.

Ideally you'll be working with a demo producer like me to create your demos. One of the jobs of a demo producer is to supply you with scripts. It's my *job* to help you understand what reads will work well with your voice and to select scripts (just for you) from my massive file-bank of scripts. Whoever you work with, this info to follow will help you to be in control of the script process.

Make sure the scripts are topical & current (you don't want to sample a Hasbro toy that has been out of production for seven years). Pick something good for your sound & style. **You never want to use anything "local" in origin.** Joe Schmo's Tire & Auto located at 12 Main Street in Springtown will not do at all. Local ads are usually poorly written and do not give you a chance to stretch your acting legs. Also, local spots have little to no credibility. **In order to compete effectively with more experienced talent, you must have a demo that is as polished as theirs. Only national and regional copy will make this possible.**

Find copy that matches the emotions you handle best. Demos are often 'faked'. Just because a commercial for a major retailer appears on a talent's demo it doesn't necessarily mean they were paid to record it. We're not lying to people or trying to con them, we're just providing examples of what we can do.

If you are questioned about the origins of a commercial on your demo or are asked if the work presented is work that you have actually been hired or paid to do; the answer should promptly be no. Instead explain that you're only trying to give an example of the type of work you are capable of. There is nothing wrong with that, especially in the early stages of your career.

If you are lucky enough to have had some previous experience, you can include well selected bits & pieces of that material for use in your demo.

Do not include any spots or audio that includes another same sex voice. And be careful of badly written dialogue copy between a man & woman. Sometimes those are more harmful than anything else, mainly because they are usually the most unnatural, unlikely scenarios. The best actor in the world can't make bad dialog sound good.

And again, don't use local spots. Main Street Deli or Tony's Pizza aren't going to make you competitive – even if you've been paid to record those commercials. Use national & regional spots with recognizable name brands & companies.

Let's say you've done a commercial for your local Goodyear Tire & Auto Service Center. Even though it may be a local commercial, the national name still carries a lot of merit. A good producer may be able to manipulate the audio & remove local references.

Also, never be afraid to re-record something you've previously done. In your

early years, you will grow & improve rapidly. If you have a great piece of copy from a commercial where your read was only so-so & you think you can do it better, do it again. In the case of demo creation, the end will always justify the means.

Recording Your Demo

If you have opted to record & produce your demo yourself then these are the guidelines you should follow. If you've hired a producer these are things you should discuss with them before they start the production process.

Ask your producer to be very critical & to help you wherever they can. You should trust their opinion & want them to be honest about your performance. Feedback is critical when behind the mic.

Always record each piece to your demo a few different ways. Read more material than you will need. The average demo recording session is an hour. That means you are recording 60 minutes of material to create a 60 second presentation.

Each piece that makes up your demo will be between 10 & 15 seconds on average. But don't just read 10 or 15 seconds worth of copy from a 60 second script. Read most or the entire script as part of the demo recording process. Then let the producer select the best 10 to 15 seconds from the read. It is how it would be done had the commercial been a paid job that you decided to put on your demo. The end result will be a more believable demo.

Don't necessarily expect to record your demo in one session. Take your time. Listen to the final takes & make sure you are selecting the best reads. Don't feel rushed or pressured to accept a read you don't think is all that great. Sometimes the pieces you expected to be fantastic end up being bad. Accept it & move on by selecting a better performance, or consider rerecording the script until you are satisfied.

If possible record the individual pieces of your demo differently by using different microphones & different compression or EQ settings. This also lends to a more believable demo. Demos are traditionally created by picking bits & pieces from audio you have been paid to perform. Those original pieces would have been recorded & mixed in different settings & at different times so they would not all sound the same.

Be careful when selecting sound effects. Stay away from harmonizers, echoes, reverb & pitch changers - basically anything that alters your natural sound dramatically. **A demo must be an accurate representation of your raw voice. Your clients will expect you to deliver whatever they hear on your demo.** Leave the audio tricks to the client. They will recognize what effects can enhance your voice once they hire you for their project.

This is not to say that a little compression, post-enhancement, or "audio boost" is unacceptable. Adding a little more bass to your voice or tweaking the recording to make your sound a little brighter is perfectly fine. Consult with your producer on what will work best. However do not "gate the compressor" so heavily that it clips the audio. Your producer will understand what this means. If they don't – find a new producer.

Make sure that no other element of the demo drowns out or overpowers your voice. Make sure all pieces are of an even volume as well. Never accept the final production if something just doesn't sound right – that's why a good producer, someone versed in audio for advertising is so crucial.

Take a preview copy home & listen to it over & over & over. Play it for your wife, mother, daughter, son, friend, co-worker, dog & cat. Get the opinions of those you trust. Ask them: "Would you hire me based on what you're hearing?" Use this review time to make any final adjustments.

Be careful not to bring too many cooks to the pot though. VO is very subjective & everyone is going to have a different opinion. Even industry professionals will have conflicting opinions about a demo.

What you are looking for is sound input, regarding the quality of the audio & the clarity of your voice and the quality of your performance.

Play the demo in your car, your home stereo, & your computer. You want to hear how the demo sounds when played from multiple sources to check the overall volume mix. Just because it sounds great at the producer's studio doesn't mean much – it was created there & the initial excitement of hearing it might affect your judgment. Clients listen to demos on a computer and since most computer speakers are very basic you want to make sure that your demo still sounds great when played through a less professional system.

After the demo is complete keep a master copy on CD or as a digital .wav. An MP3 is good to have for electronic sending but is generally not good for a master. The quality is not high enough.

You'll need between 25 & 50 physical demo copies throughout the course of a year. The majority will be sent digitally via email; so just burn individual copies as you need them. You'll want to have a few on-hand in case you're asked for one on-the-spot while out networking etc. The remainder will likely be for agents and casting directors that *still* ask for snail-mail copies.

Demo labels should be professional in appearance. Be as creative as you like, but keep it simple and easy to read. Always include contact info on both the CD face & on the case.

It usually doesn't take long before you start feeling a little dissatisfied with your current demo. **Professional VO people usually change & update their demos once a year or once every two years at the latest.** When the urge strikes you will want to change your demo fast.

Please understand that from the day it is created, you're demo is a ticking bomb. Usually an F-bomb, because the second you realize it's outdated or not a good reflection of your current sound, or that it's not trendy anymore…etc., that will probably be the expletive of choice.

For the fledgling voice talent, the creation of your first demo is often times the step that helps you to realize whether or not "Joe Smith voice-for-hire…" is officially open for business. If you feel that you are, then proceed with pride & start sending out your shiny new demo. You will be able to start gauging the effectiveness of your demo within 3 to 6 months of starting to send it to potential clients.

If you're getting work, obviously you've done well. When you are getting no response or very little, you may want to take a closer look at your demo; it might not be as great as you thought. Getting feedback from those you send your demo to for work is nearly impossible. Few people want to talk to a "newbie" about the quality & effectiveness of their demo. Remember; society teaches us that if we have nothing good to say, then we shouldn't say anything at all. Voiceover actors and coaches will have a never-ending stream of potential feedback, some of which may come with an agenda. Others will legitimately try to assist you.

Provided you have followed the guidelines in this book, your demo is probably technically sound. So, if it does not bring in the bucks, chances are it was your performance that fell short of the mark. Production & presentation count for much but ultimately it is *performance* that makes or breaks you.

If you feel that you're demo is not ready or that it failed, don't panic or give up. Sadly many talents don't find out where their skill level falls until they have attempted their first demo. Do not be discouraged.

Ideally you will be working with a coach and will not even attempt a first demo until your coach tells you that you're ready to create one. But that is not the case for everyone. Perhaps, you already have you're first demo. I'm also quick to tell my students that everyone's first demo sucks. But we ALL started somewhere. Very, very few of us have an outstanding first demo.

See, a failed demo as another part of the learning process. Use it to accurately define & recognize where you need more improvement & take the necessary steps to correct problem areas. There is hope, but it will require the help of a professional voiceover coach.

Before you begin creating a demo for yourself take time to listen to the demos the pros are putting out. VoiceHunter.com houses demos from top of the line professionals and another great tool is Voicebank.net. Voicebank is used throughout the VO industry & since many talent agents use it to showcase and promote their VO roster, the demos are excellent.

Chapter 6 – Marketing & Business

Going Into Business

Voiceover is the business of creating the "illusion of reality" for an audience. As a voiceover artist, you have the ability to make money selling & marketing the most unique product on the planet: you.

You are on the brink of becoming an entrepreneur. You are embarking on a journey that includes all the trials & joys that anyone would experience if they started their own company.

This book will not teach you how to set up & legally run a sole-proprietorship, LLC or corporation. There are plenty of websites, books, & government agencies that will assist with those processes. In this chapter we will cover the necessary elements of a successful voiceover company: sales, marketing & public relations. For further reading on this subject you'll also want to reference my voiceover business book, titled <u>How To Set-up & Maintain A BETTER Voiceover Business.</u>

As with all forms of show business money is the name of the game in VO. While you are not a commercial property, you are an item to be bought & sold, a commodity – meaning that you have a certain value. To your clients, you represent an investment. Therefore, proper presentation of you, your demo, marketing materials, & correspondence is essential for you to show your worth.

The competition is fierce; you don't want to lose credibility or a job because of typos or a faulty CD. You also want the world to know that you're serious about what you're doing – act like a pro & you'll be treated like one. But leave any doubts about your professionalism & it could be impossible to reestablish a line of communication with a potential source of work.

Always be honest & upfront about your experience level, your strengths & your weaknesses. At the same time, try to not admit to being brand new! A *student* of any profession is not desirable or hirable and you must always remember that. Voiceover clients are less concerned with how long you've been doing this and more concerned with how well you know what you're doing. Aptitude is important. Experience is not. Yet, most people still don't want to work with a rookie, so keep that info private whenever possible.

No matter how much experience you gain or how quickly you progress, there is always someone out there who knows more than you, & has more experience. They will easily see through any façade you may put on. This is typically the case with experienced voiceover buyers like advertising agencies, production companies and executive producers. So, opt for a humble approach with these clients. There's nothing wrong with saying; "I don't know the answer to that question, but give me a little time and I'll get back to you with an answer." Or you can try asking for their advice and expertise, "If you were me, what would you charge for this project?"

Gather the tools you need, understand why you need them & obtain them in a timely & cost effective manner, & you're well on your way. I'm going to give you options in this chapter. Not every method works for everyone & no two voice people are alike – (yeah we're a lot like snowflakes). Over time & with some minor trial & error, you'll learn what works best for you.

This is also a good time to note that there are investments beyond building a studio to become a voice artist. Demos cost money, as do websites and other marketing material. And don't forget that time & money are both investments. It is all part of the overhead you would expect with any business venture.

Voiceover is the business of creating the "illusion of reality" for an audience.

Marketing

Promotions, marketing, & branding are topics that keep most CEOs up at night. How potential customers see & view your name & services is a large part of success. New marketing "formulas" seem to pop-up every day. There are whole sections of book-stores dedicated to the topic. Whenever a company comes up with a new marketing concept everyone wants to know what it is & how they did it.

Marketing is about spending money to make more money. The most successful, professional voiceover people put at least 15% of their total yearly earnings back into marketing. In the beginning you may need to put 100% of anything you earn towards your marketing.

In order to create a successful marketing campaign you have to study the 3 Commandments of Marketing. Know Thy Services, Know Thy Customers, & Know Thy Competition. Ask yourself:

What does my name, my brand, my company (my voice) sound & look like?

How do I communicate those ideas quickly & easily to potential clients?

What is important to a potential client & how do I appeal to them?

How can I reach the largest number of potential clients & spend the least amount of time / money doing it?

What is my competition doing?

Your answers to these questions will change from year to year & will become more complex over time. As you start to find a niche for yourself in the voice industry, you may also need to streamline these questions to the specific types of clients for whom you work. This is not beginner information either. It is the same process we recommend to established VO talent.

To effectively market yourself you'll also need:

EMAIL – You must have a reliable form of email that you can check & access often. Become proficient in proper email etiquette & make sure that your email has a "signature". Email is not only the preferred business method of communication; it is also the preferred way to send & receive audio for VO.

BUSINESS CARDS – They should accurately describe your sound & the type of voiceover services you offer (commercial, narration, etc.), while making a strong brand or positioning statement, & details on how to reach you.

PAPER – Thank you cards, envelopes & invoices. Many are optional. All should have your logo, but at the very least your name, telephone numbers & email in a neat, easy-to-read font. Many of these items can be made from Microsoft templates found online. Vista Print is also a great service to procure postcards and business cards but DON'T use a pre-existing template – you must modify their designs extensively or build something completely custom.

A CELL PHONE - Your voice message should be friendly & professional on a business level. It should not sound like a home or personal greeting but it also shouldn't be a sales pitch – keep it simple & to the point & PLEASE – <u>smile</u> while you are recording it.

AN APPOINTMENT BOOK – desk calendar or electronic means by which to keep track of your daily schedule & goals. Microsoft Outlook or a similar program is perfect. Performer Tracker is an outstanding tool and most tablets or smart phones have plenty of apps that can help.

DEMOS – Your demos are your most important tools. (We discussed how to create stellar demos in Chapter 5.) Or contact me at my website GabrielleNistico.com for demo creation assistance.

A WEBSITE – It's a great way to showcase all of your info, house demos and in today's marketplace it legitimizes your company. Literally, no website…equals no respect. Some sites can also serve as a way for your clients to access audio, auditions & demos that you upload. They can point, click & download what they need. Consult with different parties before creating a website, preferably with companies that specialize in building websites for voiceover actors. There are many right and wrong ways to go about a web presentation in voiceover. GabrielleNistico.com can help.

Websites can be very costly and many free tools simply don't offer the professionalism needed. I *do not* recommend DIY design tools from GoDaddy, WordPress, or Weebly. Check out Wix.com and Snappages – these tools are great even if you aren't web or design savvy.

I am a big fan of DIY in general because it allows you to be in control of your own site. Dependency is bad for business and sadly many business owners are extremely dependant on their web designers for the smallest of web updates. Voiceover actors cannot afford that. When we need changes made to our sites we need them now, not two weeks from now. I own, operate and maintain all my sites; I recommend that you attempt the same. You may only need to bring in a designer to help with setting everything up or creating graphics.

A PHOTO – It doesn't have to be professional necessarily, just a clean, fun shot of you that captures a bit of your personality & that helps you to accurately represent your sound. If you don't look the way you sound, **skip the photo**. If you are a 50 year old woman but you have a very young sound (20 or younger), don't include a photo. It's unlikely that you look 20. Remember, marketing is about creating an image. You don't want your brand to contradict itself. All your public images must match your sound. Many voiceover actors (myself included), forego a picture on our websites. I want clients to believe that The Voiceover Vixen looks however they want her to. So you won't find a picture of me anywhere on VoiceoverVixen.com.

A BIO – Can be a short description of who you are & what you've done. Update it often to include your latest projects & clients. This is not a resume – a resume is not needed when looking for voiceover work. It is perceived as unprofessional & uninformed to send / submit a traditional resume as part of your marketing. It leaves people thinking you're out of work & looking for a permanent position. Or they may mistake you for an on-camera actor.

Your voiceover bio should briefly describe your voice, list any voice coaches you have trained with as well as workshops or seminars you have attended. It should also list clients that you've worked for. It may also include any professional experience apart from VO that is valuable to your VO niche.

Your bio should not be a detailed account of your entire life, where you went to school, and or a detailed account of your professional experience outside of voiceovers. Stick to the things that relate to voiceover and the sound or style you offer. Those are the things that book jobs, not your alma mater.

CREATIVE MARKETING MATERIAL – Labels, post-it-notes, folders & more. Sky's the limit. Invest in fun, useful things - a pen with your name & logo, magnets, even a tin of mints. Something that will keep your name at the top of someone's mind! Desktop items work very well & can be purchased through companies like National Pen.

Promotional items are not mandatory but they are helpful. Justification is very important. It's easy to get carried away and buy lots of promotional items. Avoid this temptation. You should only invest in these items if you can justify the expense or save for the investment via a percentage of money you have earned from paying voiceover jobs.

Personality

You are in charge of your attitude at all times. There are no excuses for poor conduct. This business is all about relationships & maintaining those relationships to the best of your ability. It's not always *what* you know but *who* you know. Never burn a bridge because someday you might need to get across it.

Forget notions of competition & cutthroat behavior; there's plenty of work to go around, so don't think of other talent as competition, think of them as allies. Voice people share work – a lot! Right now you need all the tips & tricks you can get from talent with more experience.

VoiceoverUniverse.com, Voice-overs.com, VOBB.com, Voiceover Extra.com, Voiceover Insider, Yahoo Voiceover message boards, Meet-Up Groups, and social networks provide opportunity for you to meet & mingle with other talent and make friends. (For a complete list of groups, organizations and clubs see *Step 1* on VOPrep.com) visit There are also a number of voiceover conventions in LA, Atlanta, Chicago and a few traveling events that give you a chance for industry face time It's important to have at least a few fellow talent whom you trust and can turn to for advice. Other VO talent will be able to assist you with questions pertaining to clients & their needs, what to charge for a job, technical problems and troubleshooting and so much more.

No matter how unreasonable they can seem at times, the clients are always right. Expect a good bit of criticism in the beginning. You may think you did your best & then they ask you to do it again. Or worse they tell you "that sucked!" It happens to the best of us. Just smile & do the VO again. It's not personal, it's only business.

Every voiceover actor has at least one great story about the "client from Hell". The job is a terrible mess; they are making you nervous because they are hyper-critical & seem to hate everything you do.

You've recorded dozens of takes and by the end of the session it feels as if they are settling with what they have because they just don't like you & the whole time you are wondering why in the world they hired you in the first place. You are relieved when the job is over and wonder if they will actually pay you because they seemed so dissatisfied.

A few weeks later a check arrives. A few days after that the same client calls to book you for *another* session! This can't be! Why on earth are they calling again? Turns out, they *LOVED* what you did. Second time around you are simply more prepared for their rude, persnickety behavior. Odds are pretty good you were calling back, in-part, due to the graceful way you handled the first experience with this client. Many talent would not be able to maintain their cool in the same situation. Clients can and will push your buttons. Stay calm and voiceover on.

If you claim to be a professional you owe it to yourself to be just that – professional. In many cases the reliable, moderately talented pro will get more work than the temperamental VO genius. Why? A temperamental talent is an unreliable talent & an unreliable talent is costly to the client.

Beware of the ego that lurks in the deepest recesses of your mind. Let's face it - you like to be in the spotlight. If you didn't you wouldn't be pursuing what is ultimately a career in the entertainment industry. You may be a humble student now, but wait & see how your ego swells after a few great gigs.

Never brag & always be thankful for the work you receive. Catering to prima donnas can no longer be tolerated in today's cost-conscious adverting industry. But at the end of the day feel free to look in the mirror & say with pride – "I am the best. I am a genius. I am going to take over the world one VO at a time!"

Personality Check (List)

YOU ARE IN CHARGE OF YOUR ATTITUDE - Keep it light & cheery & have fun on a professional level.

NEVER CRITICIZE, GOSSIP OR BAD MOUTH – You'll sound bitter. We are a shockingly small industry. Sometimes it feels as if everyone knows *everyone*. Be discreet; don't put yourself in an awkward position.

NEVER CARRY A GRUDGE - Forgive & move on. Learn from experiences & accept that people are sometimes (insert the expletive of your choice). No matter your personal opinion, you should be able to respect everyone in this industry for their business accomplishments at the very least.

DON'T GET FRUSTRATED WITH CLIENTS - They can sometimes be rude or confusing. You'll be amazed by how few of them understand the industry & how demanding they can be. Be friendly & firm. Help them, guide them & teach them. They'll appreciate it later and you'll be rewarded with recurring work.

ALWAYS SAY IT WITH A SMILE – Make sure you sound happy, friendly, warm, caring, etc. Speak clearly & articulate over the phone.

DON'T CONDUCT BUSINESS IN A BAD MOOD – If your patience has been tested, relax & take the time you need to regroup & be in a better place. Moody & "actor" shouldn't be synonymous. You are a business owner *first*, remember that.

EVERY NO PUTS YOU ONE STEP CLOSER TO A YES – All performers hear the word "no" a lot. Voiceover actors are no exception. Rejection is a big part of this business. Don't let naysayers discourage you. Be persistent.

BE POSITIVE – Don't be a Debbie Downer. Keep personal matters personal and make sure that you're work relationships see you as a constant optimist.

Dress to Impress

One of the greatest things about our industry is that suits & ties need not apply. You are an *artist,* a person full of self-expression, & you're expected to dress that part. What the world doesn't know is that most of us work at home & we're lucky if we ever make it out of our pajamas. But when you do leave your abode for business, how should you look?

Business casual is fine but voiceover actors can be a bit more eccentric. Don't look like you're going to the beach, but board room attire is not necessary. You're going to an audition, a casting call, a recording session or a creative session. Whatever you wear you need to feel comfortable & confident. Expect that you'll be performing. You want to look good & not feel self-conscious about a coffee stain on your shirt. Also, many clients will be endeared to you if you are a vibrant muse. Many voiceover actors are known (and respected) for their irreverent t-shirt collection, silly shoes, a broad selection of hats or a particular, signature article of clothing.

Comfort also plays an important role in recording & microphone technique. Good luck getting enough air into your diaphragm if you're squeezed into a one-size-too-small suit. You'll be gasping for air midway through the session & the studio engineer will wonder if you left your oxygen tank at home. Likewise, standing at a microphone for hours on end is no fun in murderously high heels just because they matched your super-cute new skirt; trust me.

Noisy clothing is a big no-no. Dangly, jingly jewelry, watches that beep unexpectedly, squeaky shoes, corduroy pants and anything else that makes excessive amounts of noise will be heard on mic. Be conscious of wanting to fidget with clothes and accessories, too.

Use your best judgment when it comes to dress. There will always be the exception; like an ultra-casual business lunch at the local diner. Or you might find that you've been asked to attend a dinner party that celebrates a successful ad campaign that featured your voice. Know where you're going, who you're meeting, and if you're expected to be in the recording booth; it will help you to gauge.

Details are what set you apart from the rest of the unorganized, creative geniuses. The more organized & prepared you are to conduct business, the more success you'll have in voiceovers. Actors & VO talent are generally notorious for being chaotic and very poor with managerial skills.

Take an honest self inventory. Are you organized or are you a clutter-bug? Do you always know the location of you're most important legal and tax documents, or does a spouse or significant other keep track of those things? Do you tend to start projects but never finish them? Is it time you learned the ways of the obsessive compulsives, my child? OCD can and will be your friend.

Always carefully review anything that is about to leave your hands. Proof-read all emails & correspondence. Listen to the demo or audition you're about to send, and make sure it's free of errors & glitches. Even professionally recorded & duplicated CDs sometimes contain mistakes. In the words of my silly but *brilliant* voice-actress friend, Lisa Biggs, "A.B.C. – always be checkin'!"

Make sure the person you're sending your material to is the right person & not a receptionist or someone in the wrong department. Follow up with a postcard, phone call, letter, or email. Whatever you're most comfortable with. If they haven't listened to your demo yet, call every few weeks until they do. And remember to request feedback on the audio you send. It's the only way to know if you're meeting the needs of the companies hiring talent. Three times is the charm on call backs. If you have not received a response after 3 attempts it is not wise to continue to call that person.

Keep a detailed list or spreadsheet of all the contacts to whom you have sent your information. It may take up to six months to get a response & they're bound to call when you least expect it.

Always carry at least two copies of your demo on you or in your car. Always. You never know how or when you'll run into someone who can hire you, or get your demo to someone who will. Always bring multiple demo copies to auditions & recording sessions too, especially if you have recently updated your demos.

Have the courtesy to be on time for auditions & sessions. 15 minutes early is ideal. Train yourself to remember everyone's name & face.

Keep copies of all scripts & audio whether they are from auditions or paid jobs. They come in handy when updating your demo, working with a coach or when you are asked for a specific audio example.

Write thank you notes or emails to people who got you in the door, helped you get a great lead, & of course, all clients. Remember, out-of-sight means out-of-mind. You'd be amazed by how much a note of thanks is appreciated. It may sit on someone's desk for a long time acting as a reminder of your grace & gratitude. In today's electronic age it never hurts to stand out by using a more traditional means of communication, like a greeting card.

Know the terms & conditions of a job. If you agree to record a three page narration for a client & set a price accordingly, but the client then provides you with *six* pages, you must renegotiate BEFORE the recording. You can't renegotiate a deal after the fact. Deals can change in a heartbeat too. Always be prepared to make your clients aware of YOUR terms & conditions. For instance, you might say: "I'll record up to four pages for $300 but additional pages will be $125 each."

Getting Paid

The standard rates of pay for non-union VO talent are vague & subjective at best. There are some standards but they are not strongly enforced by any one party. As a result, a voice actor can charge whatever they see fit for their services & whatever a client is willing to pay, within reason of course.

Determining fair compensation for a voiceover can be tricky. There are a lot of factors that go into rate negotiations and it's critical that you have an understanding of how to self-represent, quote jobs and review offers. I'm going to offer the best advice I can based on my personal experiences as a voice talent and also as a casting director.

First, we'll go over some basics. As I've mentioned previously in this book, you should not enter the voiceover market as a beginner, or a student. Provided you have properly educated yourself in this craft there shouldn't be any discernible difference between you and someone who has been a voiceover actor for 5, 10 or even 20 years. That individual will just have more clients than you.

I get rather upset when I hear voiceover students talk about accepting "beginner's rates" or factoring their newness into the price of a job. No, no, no. A dentist fresh out of medical school does not charge less than a dentist who has been in business for 20 years. We are all actors, new and veterans alike. Therefore, we all deserve to be paid the same.

Often times new talent work for very little or even for free. The common belief is that experience is more valuable than payment for beginners. I disagree. Talent who work for free are not held to the same standards or expectations as those who charge for their services. A client that is getting work from you for free will always tell you that your work is exceptional and that they love everything you're doing. Of course they do, it's free! Who doesn't LOVE free? You'll never receive honest, usable feedback this way and therefore won't learn how to live up to professional standards.

It's acceptable to be flexible when you're new and perhaps more willing to go the extra mile for a client, but please avoid "giving it away", that's just bad business.

Likewise, try to avoid being greedy now or in the future. We are in an industry that pays us (for the most part) to have fun & to do something we all genuinely enjoy doing. Therefore nothing is more off-putting than a greedy talent. There are plenty of talent that actually say "I will not get out of bed for less than $\underline{X}$ number of dollars".

If an offer seems reasonable, take it! What is reasonable? Well if a job takes you less than an hour or two to complete & is a few hundred dollars more than you had yesterday...take the job! Only you can determine the amount of money needed to pay your bills and maintain your lifestyle.

Try breaking down the price of a job being offered to you by an hourly scale. Few working stiffs earn more than $30 an hour, so if you get a number higher than that you're doing pretty well for your time. And voiceover work almost always consistently equals $50 an hour or more.

If you do find yourself in a position of refusing work because a price is too low, then back out gracefully. Don't lecture others about how much you made last week, or that you are worth more, etc. Instead politely turn the work away. Don't leave anyone feeling like they spoke to an ego-monster.

Since all voiceover artists are freelancers (also known as independent contractors), you're not actually employed by the companies that hire you. You are providing them with a particular service that they need every so often. This means that when your work is completed you bill (or invoice) them for your services. You can expect to be paid in as few as 10 days or as many at 90 depending on the company & what their accounts payable policy is for outside vendors. In most cases you will see a check in 30 to 60 days of your invoice date.

The check you receive will not have any tax, social security or other federal or state requirements withheld. Those fees & taxes are now YOUR responsibility to pay. Freelancers, of course, do not receive benefits or medical insurance unless they pay for these things out of their own pocket.

Companies will often times ask you to provide them certain tax information before they can pay you, like a W-9 form. At the end of the year they will send you a 1099 (tax form) that you will declare to the government, paying any taxes due on the earnings. Consult with an accountant for more info on these & other standard practices of self-employed people.

At one time in each voice talent's life they get "burned" on payment, meaning that a company or individual who hired them failed to pay. In the beginning of your career this can be a harsh, even devastating lesson. It usually costs more in legal fees to recoup the loss than what is actually owed to you.

You should always require payment upfront from ANY new client. You should always require payment upfront from overseas or foreign clients as they are even harder to collect from if they fail to pay their bill.

Make sure you are capable of receiving payments via check, credit card, or bank transfer. Set up a PayPal account & your clients can easily pay you via credit card. A Square account is excellent too. After a successful first encounter, you can then allow a client to become part of a regular monthly billing cycle for all future work.

When you are committing a client to a contract or term of work, make sure the agreement is in writing & that it is legal & binding in your state & theirs. You can obtain such documents through the

Chamber of Commerce, online or through a reputable business lawyer.

Next, we will explore a general breakdown of payment by dollar amount. It will help you get a feel for what is normal & consistent with the rest of the non-union VO industry. There are, however, always exceptions. You will have to take each job case by case. Try never to shortchange yourself but also try to keep your rates within your client's available budget.

Be wary of charging too little – such activity drives down the rates for all VO talent & is never a good idea. It might seem smart to be super cheap early on so as to gain lots of clients. But the clients you attract will not be worthwhile. The industry refers to voiceover actors that do this as Bottom Feeders.

In the last decade or so – especially during and after the recession, the practices of ill-trained, novice Bottom Feeders successfully reduced voiceover rates for all non-union actors. There were simply too many people offering substandard work very cheaply. How cheap – look no further than the loathsome voiceover practices on Craig's List, Fivr, Voice Bunny and Internet Jocks, as-well-as, many pay-to-play websites such as Voice 123 & Voices.com. We'll explore pay-to-play companies in much more detail, later in this book.

For now, a word of warning; many low-budget websites such as those listed above will publically post suggested voiceover rates. NEVER use or quote those rates! In most all situations those rates are posted online to attract the attention of low-budget clients who are looking for bargain-brand voiceovers. Those rates do nothing but attract more and more low-paying jobs! But that's how these companies make a living. They don't protect the interest of the voiceover actors; they protect the interests of the low-ball clients.

Voiceovers for less than 100 Dollars

Generally jobs for less than $100 mean:

- The job is a **commercial** being used in a **small market**. Most small markets only pay about $75 per spot.

- The work is for a high-volume, low-pay client. An example would be: $25 per :30 **commercial with a written guarantee** of 5 commercials per week for 1 year.

- The job is for a very short, :30 or less **non-broadcast** job for the internet, internal use or for an over-seas client.

These examples are all classified as "low-budget". Many voiceover actors will not work for this amount as it is below a fair or standard minimum.

Some talent make a living booking work mainly in this category. They do so by volume. If you book ten $100 jobs per week that means you earn $4,000 per month before taxes. These jobs won't make you a notable voiceover actor and you won't garner the respect of your peers, but you will pay the bills.

Here are some additional low budget booking opportunities. If someone wants to pay you between three & 15 dollars per page to read & record an **audio book**, it is an average rate. Audio books are a growing area of voiceover but they don't pay very well at this time.

A **message-on-hold** script may contain six audio bits or parts. Some M.O.H companies will pay $1 to $5 dollars per bit. These pieces are small, 20 to 30 seconds each, so realistically speaking you can record about 20-30 bits in an hour. Get the client to book for an entire days worth of these things & (providing that your studio costs are minimal) the money isn't too bad.

Voiceovers for $100-$250 Dollars

Generally jobs for $100 to $250 mean:

- You are voicing a few lines, a tag, a donut or a disclaimer for a commercial to be aired regionally.

- You are recording a small **non-broadcast** project for in-house use within a company. No more than 2 pages.

- This is also the standard price paid for non-union, **broadcast commercials** in small or medium radio & TV markets.

- This is also where pricing for **non-broadcast** work in just about every venue starts for 1 to 3 pages of work.

- **Radio station & TV promo** rates begin here as well. Entry level VO talent should agree to no more than four pages a month at a rate of $200 or $250 per month. This rate is acceptable providing that the station signs a one-year contract. A more seasoned voice professional will usually only provide one page a month at this rate with a signed contract. This is for small markets only.

These rates are average or just below average for talent throughout most of the country. They are more than fair for talent with limited experience.

Voiceovers for $250-$500 Dollars

Jobs in this price range generally mean:

- This is the average monthly rate for **radio imaging or TV promo** contracts. Small markets will require a large number of monthly pages for this price. Medium markets will require two to four pages & large markets will only require a few pages at this rate.

- This is also the average price for small (under 5 pages) **industrial** or **narration** jobs where you are being asked to give a total project price as opposed to per page.

- The starting rates for most non-union foreign voiceover work since, depending on the language, foreign VO is harder to come by & pays more.

This is the starting rate for high profile, non-union, **non-broadcast** jobs as well as the base rate for low profile, large market, non-union, **broadcast** or **commercial** jobs.

If you are commanding these prices, you are doing well & you are earning the standard wages of most voiceover actors.

Rates above these amounts are generally beyond the reach of a beginner but they do go higher, much higher. Union scale rates **start** at roughly $400. Those rates can triple & beyond. Superstar voice talent can earn from $5,000 to $50,000 per booking.

As your business grows you will start to better understand rates of pay, trends in pay-scale, & the needs & wants of your clients.

Union vs. Non-Union

You are currently defined as a non-union voiceover artist. Some VO talent choose to stay non-union for the duration of their career. Others work to become unionized as fast as possible. There are pros & cons to both. Over time you will decide which is the most lucrative for you. How your career progresses will dictate whether or not you make the jump to union status.

The most important thing to keep in mind is this: Joining the union is only worthwhile & beneficial if you are capable of getting a steady stream of union work. Otherwise it could be a wasted investment.

Non-union talent are free to take any job they wish to take. There is no standardization for how they are paid & they can charge anything they see fit. The same goes when a client is hiring a non-union talent. Clients can offer a pay rate of anything they see fit. As the talent, you are solely responsible for monitoring the use of your voice & making sure that you are not being "abused".

For instance: you charge $200 for a local use, single market TV commercial in Alabama & you come to find that the audio is being aired all over the Southeast on a regional basis. You have no protection should such a thing happen & it's up to you to take any legal action against the company that unlawfully used your voice.

Everything you do as a non-union talent is called a "buy-out", unless otherwise negotiated. This means that once recorded the company paying you owns the audio & can do with it whatever they see fit. They can air the commercial for years if they like. They own the use of your voice for that particular project & you can no longer claim ownership to your own voice, unless you had your client sign a contract that states otherwise. You'll receive no residual income for extended use because you have "signed-over" your intellectual property. It's uncommon for anyone to sign a restriction contract with a non-union talent for something as small as a local radio spot.

Over 15 years ago when my voiceover career was in its infancy, I voiced a variety of commercials in my home-town, Long Island, NY. Most all those commercials were buy-outs. Still to this day you can occasionally hear my voice on spots and tags on Long Island radio & TV because some of those clients are still using those old recordings.

Insist upon a restricted one year use contract for any piece of commercial copy that is generic (in that it does not contain a date in the voiceover). Most commercials can only be used for a short period of time because they contain date-specific material and a portion of the copy may read "Come to the midyear clearance sale happening this weekend, June 16th & 17th". A commercial like this has a very short life span so a buy-out term is acceptable.

When sending an invoice for a non-union job always ask the client if you need a purchase order number (a number they will provide). Since the fees you charge will vary greatly from job to job, keep excellent records & copies of all your invoices. Non-union jobs are usually paid within 30 to 60 days; consider yourself very lucky if you receive payment earlier than that. After 30 days it is all right to start sending late notices.

Most companies will ask for "market exclusivity" when they hire you. If you are voicing spots for a furniture store in Detroit, you promise not to voice a commercial for any other furniture store in that market. New clients will make you aware of any conflicting interests at the time of your audition, so reads notes about conflicts carefully.

Radio & TV stations hiring you for imaging & promo work are the most likely to require market exclusivity. You are agreeing that you won't become the voice of any other station in that market. A station that wants market exclusivity must meet your requirements too – like signing a 12-month contract that guarantees you payment whether they use your services for the full 12 months or not.

Unless you are working with an agent or casting company that deals in non-union casting, no one else gets a percentage of what you earn when you are non-union. Whatever you charge goes to you, & you alone. The only fees you are responsible for are your taxes.

Union talents are restricted to only union work. They are not allowed to take non-union jobs unless they are Financial Core (a type of exemption status within the union). How much you get paid for a job is first & foremost dictated by the union & a starting rate of pay called "scale".

A client looking for union talent must be willing to pay at least union scale for the VO & then possibly anything above & beyond the amount that a particular talent might require. The union offers various benefits such as health insurance, pension & retirement benefits, while ensuring that you are paid properly & accordingly. The union offers legal protection & makes sure that you are paid for your work in a timely manner too. You pay "into" all of these services when you pay your union dues.

Every broadcast project you voice as a union talent is only allowed to air for a maximum of 13 weeks. Anything over 13 weeks of air-time starts to accrue residuals. The company that paid for your voice does not own the audio. Instead they lease it for a short period of time. When that lease period is up (13 weeks) they must pay you more if they intend to keep using the audio. You keep getting paid without doing any additional work. This is a luxury that many actors know & enjoy.

When getting paid for a union job, all you have to do is keep track of the work you've done & who owes you what. The union & your agent do the rest. They make sure that you are paid in a timely manner (usually within 30 days) & they even collect late fees on your behalf. Most union work is market exclusive & product type exclusive automatically, but a company pays top dollar for that privilege.

As a union actor, you trust others to play crucial roles in your career. You are trusting union reps, agents & managers to take proper actions on your behalf. This is not to say, that you should not be proactive. It is essential that you actively take part in your negotiations & deals. Do not put blind faith into agents & managers. However you should however, have a certain measure of trust in your representation team.

Everyone gets a piece of the pie. Your work is capitalized on by lots of people. The union gets a percentage, your agent gets a percentage, a signatory gets a percentage, & your manager gets some too. Each party is tacking on a certain percentage to the total amount you earn. Your $400 VO really costs a client $700. Not every client can afford that.

If you decide now or in the future that the union is right for you, you would join SAG/AFTRA. There are many eligibility requirements in order to join & there are yearly dues you must pay. Contact them to find out more.

The decision to join or not to join should not be terribly complicated. You'll most likely start off as a non-union voiceover actor and as your career progresses the industry will dictate your next move. Agents, and trusted voiceover colleagues will prompt you to join the union when / if it's time. Earnings will play a factor too; voiceover actors earning 100,000 or more annually should consider unionizing. Geography can play a role. Is there enough union work in your area to sustain a living?

And lastly the type of work you specialize in will play a big role in your decision to join or not to join. Animation actors are almost always unionized but there are many types of VO that the union does not recognize or regulate. Radio Imaging & Telephony work are currently not mandated by the union. You'll figure out what is best for you when the time is right.

Ethics & Voiceovers

Let's talk about ethics for a moment. As in most industries, they do exist. There are a few situations that VO people occasionally encounter & you should be ready for them early in your career when you are the most vulnerable.

We all know that sex sells. But when & where do we draw the line? Night clubs, bars, strip bars, "lounges", lingerie, & pornography / novelty shops often employ voice talent for commercials. Usually the copy is pretty tame & the client just wants an excessively sexual & suggestive read. No big deal. But be wary of these industries as well as porn related software companies & movie manufacturers. Moan-overs aren't exactly resume building work. A reputation as being the person that voices greetings for 900 number sex lines may not be appealing to prospective clients later.

If a voiceover job goes against everything you believe in then by all means turn the job away. You should never sacrifice your own morals. Make sure you understand the distribution of the material you are voicing & how widely it will be available to a public or consumer audience.

Secondly, make sure that nothing you voice will be considered offensive by a large number of people. Clients sometimes want to take a controversial approach to advertising in the hopes of generating "a buzz" but that doesn't mean you are obligated to partake in the process.

Try not to be involved with a project that is slanderous in a way that breaks common decency or civil rights & liberties. For example I was once asked to create a commercial for a mobile home manufacturer post 9-11. The client wanted to make fun of the then President, Iraq, Saddam Hussein, & the death of his two sons. I refused the job. The money is not worth that kind of immorality. Nothing about September 11th is funny. As a native New Yorker and the daughter of a retired Marine, I found the entire thing to be really gross.

Many voiceover actors refrain from voicing for: porn, the alcoholic beverage industry, tobacco companies, gasoline and oil companies, religious organizations and political ads for politicians.

You don't necessarily need to begin a client or agent interaction by talking about all the things you don't want to do. Just take things on a job by job basis. It can be a bit diva like to lead with your moral & ethical no-no list.

Instead, begin the conversation by talking with a client about their expectations of you. Most clients expect that when you voice their commercial you will not voice for a similar company in the immediate area. This is not exclusivity per say but it is a professional courtesy to avoid conflicts. A sort of "unwritten" rule.

If you have previously recorded for a Furniture Store in Cleveland & their competitor also wants to hire you then you need to let the newer, potential client know that you have done work for his competition in the past. If this doesn't bother him then call your existing client & let them know what is happening. Allow it to be their choice as to whether or not you take the new job. It's only fair.

Keeping your word & being honest in this business is especially important. People are depending on you to meet your deadlines & deliver a quality product. Be honest about time frame, deadlines, & when people can expect to have material back from you.

Your skills & the services you offer are a vital part of the advertising industry. Treat the industry well, conduct yourself like a professional, respect yourself & your success will not be far behind.

Chapter 7 – Finding Voiceover Work

Seemingly, the hardest part of the VO industry is finding work. However it's not that difficult. With proper planning and strategy it can actually be rather easy to receive consideration for VO work. We will now explore a number of conventional & unconventional ways to get your name & demo to potential clients.

We always recommend starting small. You're going to make mistakes in the beginning. You may not have all the answers or the right responses & you might be nervous or unsure at first. It's better to "goof" with the small fish than with the big fish. Besides, finding the small fish is easy & will give you plenty of practice so that you are ready & prepared to reel in the big ones later.

Keep your eyes & ears open for opportunities that surround your day-to-day life. Start to look at the area you live in a little differently & you'll be surprised at how many potential sources of income you might find.

In the beginning, be sure to not only keep an eye out for paid opportunities but trade as well. You'll be surprised by how many places of business will trade their goods or services for yours. Even though you won't be paid cash, you're gaining experience. Hopefully, you'll be getting something useful that you would have purchased anyway. But please note this is not the same as working for free! Your voiceover should always come with a dollar value, even if you allow a trade to take place.

One of the first things you need to do is look at your current life & work experience. It is very possible that your current or past occupation & hobbies may have more to do with VO than you realize. You will find the transition into a voice career easier if you have some area of expertise that you can use as a stepping stone into voiceover work.

Take a moment to assess your life. Do you have ties to any of the following professions or industries: Medical, Dental, Automotive, Computers, Education, Child Care, Retail Sales, Home Improvement, Real Estate, Banking or Hospitality? Do your hobbies include: Sports, Charitable Organizations, a Church, Clubs, Parks & Recreation, Travel or Dining? Almost all of these (and more) can & do use the services of voiceover talent.

Many people who come from a medical background find great success in VO by first marketing their services to doctor's offices, nursing schools, & pharmaceutical companies. Those with automotive sales experience or mechanical knowledge may want to market their voice to car dealers, repair shops, & tire centers as well as technical voiceovers within the Explainer Video market.

This is an important step in starting to think like an entrepreneur, & will ease some of the pressure & anxiety of pursuing a new career path. By starting with something you already know & understand, you'll be more at ease.

Short of sounding like an Amway affiliate, the next part of your early marketing plan should include your family & friends. Everyone you know should be made aware of your new endeavor, even co-workers & the parents of your children's friends. You never know who can lead to work. Give a few copies of your demo to friends & family for passing to others.

Everything that involves recorded audio of almost any kind is a voiceover. If your kid's best friend's father owns a local car dealership, maybe he needs someone to record a professional sounding greeting on his phone system. You never know until you start to talk to the people closest to you. Don't be afraid to make suggestions as to who they might speak with on your behalf. For that matter, it's never a bad idea to write things down for them & tell them exactly what to say to others.

I believe that friends and family want to help but so rarely do they understand what we do for a living. My assistance and close friend Lewis Banks officially launched his voiceover business in early 2014. His grandmother is still waiting for his first rap album to come out!

While it may be hard to help Grandma understand the intricacies of voiceover, it won't be with most of the rest of your friends and family. Make a list of everyone you know. *Everyone*. Include their name, profession and the likelihood of them having a direct connection to voiceover work. Use Facebook, (and other social media) email, and phone calls to speak with them one-on-one about your new business endeavor. Then task them with something simple: "Can you get me the name and number of your company's marketing director?" Or, "Can you take my demo directly to your boss and let him know that we're good friends?"

Local businesses that you associate with are also great resources for early work. Does your dentist or family doctor have a poorly recorded, unprofessional sounding message-on-hold? Suggest that you record a new one for them. Does your gym do a lot of radio advertising? Ask to speak with the owner or manager, give him a copy of your demo. Even if they are "satisfied" with their current audio provider, let them know that you'll do the job for less than what they currently pay – that's a guaranteed way to get their attention.

Never speak poorly of a company's current audio or provider. Especially when you're suggesting they change it. For all you know that could be the owner's wife delivering that horrible message-on-hold. Instead talk about the benefits of working with you.

How about your church, or a not-for-profit club or organization that you dedicate your time to? Audio for these types of businesses are most often known as public service announcements or P.S.A.s. They don't usually pay well, but they are a great way to gain experience.

Another excellent way to gain work & meet local business owners is to join the local chamber of commerce. You'll be able to introduce them to the valuable service you provide with minimal intimidation. You never know who you might meet & who might hire you on the spot. Business to Business relations are the cornerstone of most service-oriented companies. Make no mistake about it; you are a service provider.

Believe it or not, telemarketing is one of the best things you can do to start getting VO work & you'll learn a lot from the process! The first place to start is the local phone book or online equivalent. Look for: advertising agencies, recording facilities, audio / visual production companies, television program producers, on-hold message companies, book publishers (see if they have an audio publishing department) and casting companies.

If you live in a small area & can't find many places in your area, just internet search the closest city or metropolitan area.

Set a daily goal for a certain number of calls. Keep a list of all those contacted, as well as the date you called. You can expect that you may be calling people numerous times & leaving messages before getting a response to your questions. Here's what you are calling to ask:

"Do you accept voiceover demos from actors & voiceover people?" If they say no, don't simply end the call. Ask if they deal with audio production for radio, TV, on-hold & the like. If they say yes, it means the jobs are being outsourced to a production company that works with them to fulfill orders for their clients. Politely ask if they can give you the name & number of the company they use or if they can recommend who you might send a demo to. Often times, this will yield valuable information & lead you to your next call.

"Do you have your own in-house recording facility or studio?"
This is important to know because this tells you whether you might travel to their facility to record. If they say they use an outside facility, find out who it is. That company will be your next call. When you call that company you'll explain that so-&-so from such-&-such suggested you call & get info about who to send a demo to. This is called a referral & by way of introduction means the party on the other end will be more likely to talk to you since they will recognize the name you just dropped.

"Whom should I send a demo to?" Get detailed information – such as title & department. Also ask for this person's email address.

"Could you confirm your mailing address for me?" Again, be detailed. It's not a bad idea to ask how they prefer to receive demos. Most will say email; some will say regular mail.

"What sort of audio production does your company provide?" Ask what kind of audio they deal in the most - radio, TV, on-hold messages, industrials, web audio, etc. - & make a note of it.

The only exception to your telemarketing venture will be radio & TV stations. Stations do not like outside voice artists for the purpose of commercials & everyday audio. They have in-house people who are paid a steady salary for the purpose of fulfilling those needs. Radio & TV stations do however, hire outside people for the purpose of imaging. If this type of work interests you and once you have an imaging or TV Promo demo, then you would call & ask for the name of the station's Program Director, Operations Manager (if they have one) & Creative Services or Production Director.

Get the email addresses of all of these people as well as a physical mailing address. Send your demo to them all. Wait about a week & then email to inquire if & when they might be looking for a new imaging voice. Please ask them to keep you in mind when that time comes. Also, try to target stations that have a format for which your voice is well suited. Radio & TV formats vary greatly & voice talent cannot be all things to all people.

Stations usually hire imaging voices on a contract or retainer basis, so you may have to wait until their current contract comes to a close before they'll be interested in speaking with a new voice person. Be patient; timing is everything when it comes to stations.

It's important that you sound confident and self-assured when calling companies about your voiceover services. The worst thing you can do is sound desperate when looking for VO work. There is a stench of desperation that people can hear and feel when you call them. It's a major turn-off. Also, it's not advantageous to sound like a salesperson when you call. Business people and consumers alike shy away from anyone who is blatantly trying to sell them something.

Instead of a stiff sales pitch try for a more casual and inviting approach. We find that business to business propositions are best presented when you approach the situation as one business owner taking the time to inquire with another business owner about a mutually beneficial relationship. This allows each party to feel a need for the other.

Once you have mastered the local scene & feel as though you have bugged every source of work in town, the next step is to reach beyond your local borders. Remember you are not geographically limited in VO. Your hometown might not play any role in your long-term voiceover career.

There are many different publications, & websites that specialize in voiceovers. You can search for most of these resources online & you should also seek out business related directories & websites. Some recommended companies are VORG.com, AllAccess.com,

Call Sheet, Craig's List, Guru.com, MerchantCircle.com., LinkedIn, Mandy.com, ProductionHub, and Showbiz Weekly.

The web is a voiceover person's greatest resource. Your mission is to search for anyone & everyone that will accept your demo. Voice artists work for people all over the country that they may never meet in person. The industry has taken an amazing direction allowing talent to broaden their marketability nationwide. If you think you are ready for that step, here's what you need to know:

Focus primarily on advertising agencies & production houses. However, typing "advertising agency" into a search engine like BING yields over 50 million websites. Set a daily or weekly goal so that you don't become overwhelmed. You don't need to contact all of them. Learn to narrow your search for agencies that deal primarily in audio production. Try starting with just your state & expand from there. You'll need more experience before sending your demos to ad agencies in cities as large as New York or Los Angeles.

Social network websites like Facebook are also great ways to find & meet new sources of work. Use sites like Twitter to keep everyone updated on your business.

It will take a few years, but once you've started to make a name for yourself and you've started earning a reasonable income, it will be time to contact agents and inquire about representation.

Hollywood **Agents** take a percentage of everything you earn but they take care of all legal matters & paperwork. However, getting a high-powered agent in New York or Los Angeles is not easy. They only want to work with the best & most capable talent – those that will get lots of work. After all, that's how they make money.

There are smaller agents throughout much of the country & you are allowed to have more than one agent. Many talent have representation in every region in the country.

Everyone wants an agent. But sometimes I think talent want an agent for the wrong reasons. In all the years that I have worked with talent & talent agents I have found that the talent who have excellent working relationships with their agents are those that set realistic goals with regard to their representation. It's all about expectation management.

You should see your agent (or a potential agent) as someone who can negotiate excellent rates & terms on your behalf & someone who will increase your exposure & get you auditions. Your agent should also assist you with advice on your demos, auditions & over-all presentation. And lastly your agent should be someone who can add to your credibility as a professional talent.

Your agents are NOT the Holy Grail of work. Many talent make the mistake of thinking a good agent is all it takes to be successful & that once they have a reputable agent, the burden of success is in the agent's hands. That is not so, your agent is a part of your team, but you still need to be proactive in your business.

When seeking an agent you must present a clean, well put together package. Keep it simple and say the bare minimum in written form. Nothing will matter as much as the demo they hear. Visually, the package should be graphically stunning. Don't bug agents with a myriad of follow-up calls and emails either.

I've written a small pocket guide book on how to get and keep a voiceover agent; check it out for more info on the subject. You have a little time before you need to worry too much about the subject of booking an agent. You have to train with a coach and have all your marketing material (including demos) ready, before you approach them.

Down the line, you'll also want to build relationships with:

Managers: A manager acts alone or in conjunction with your agent to negotiate terms, contract details & payment for your VO jobs.

The best managers only work for a few talent at a time & are very selective about the talent they work with.

Managers also assist you with time management and take on the role of financial advisor. Sometimes a manager will also aid you in marketing.

Producers: They are responsible for finished audio / video projects. Most times, they work for an end-client, but they can hire you. Make friends with them because if they like you they will hire you often. Usually they are affiliated with a recording studio or ad agency & have access to multiple clients that could hire you.

In addition, producers are highly sought out & move somewhat frequently for better job opportunities. They are very loyal to talent they enjoy working with. A producer will take his preferred voice talent "with him" to any new company or opportunity that might arise. They are in it for the long haul, the same as you. If a producer hires you for work and your performance is good, you will make that producer look great to the client.

Voiceover Marketplaces & pay-to-play websites: There are online companies that act as large directories & bid sites for talent & VO jobs. Their costs vary. They offer you a presence on the web along with thousands of other talent. Some of these companies are auction style and you bid for voice jobs. Others allow clients to post a need for a talent & you are able to respond to the advertisement. Voices.com, Voice123.com, Bodalgo.com, CommercialVoices.com, VoiceoverArtistes.com, & VoPlanet.com are examples of these sites.

Talent experience varying degrees of success with these services. Are they worth giving a try? Yes. Should they be the only way in which you receive job opportunities? No. Pay to Play websites are not concerned with the success or failure of the talent they list. Most are not selective either, so anyone willing to pay a listing fee may join regardless of experience level or quality.

I always marvel at the number of beginner voiceover talent who join pay-to-play websites prematurely. There is a belief that these sites offer plenty of 'practice' opportunities for beginners. I believe, if you are paying hundreds of dollars to join a site where professionals are competing for work, you'd better be capable of more than practice. You can receive dozens of audition opportunities a day from sites like Voice.com and Voice123.com. However, if you don't have a quality studio of your own, or professional demos, or audition training, you won't be hirable or competitive.

Some auditions that come from pay-to-play websites will be very worthwhile and others will be sub-standard work that isn't worth the time it takes to audition. About 40% of the auditions are great, the rest are not. You should be very selective when answering marketplace / pay-to-play auditions. In the last few months I have received over 700 auditions from the Voice123 service. I've only applied for 30 of them.

I caution all of my students to research, review, take classes on, and really understand pay-to-play sites before investing in them. There are many disgruntled individuals (mostly on the web) who have had very bad experiences with these services. I think many of these talent's issues and grievances could have been avoided had they better understood pay-to-play sites before spending money. Both J. Michael Collins (one of, if not *the* most successful talent on pay-to-play sites) and I, offer pay-to-play training. Our approaches are very different, yet both are very effective. Look up J. to learn more and tell him I said 'hey'.

In general, the amount of voiceover work you will receive depends entirely upon how much time you can & will put into finding work.

It's important to know that since you are not embarking on traditional job hunting; your success is also greatly dependant on the relationships you develop. A close friend and successful TV producer once wisely said "I paid my tuition for broadcasting school not so much for the education, but for the networking it provided me." He was very right.

Only a few months after graduation, he was far ahead of his classmates with job opportunities & connections. He accomplished this because he made it a point to build a relationship with every faculty member, advisor & guest speaker that had something to do with his education.

Relationship building is equally important in voiceovers. Taking the time to meeting with people face to face, build friendships over the phone & the internet & maintaining a 'social' business will greatly impact your success. So will tenacity, ambition and an all-around great attitude that exudes confidence and passion.

I'm often asked to share stories about my students who are examples of success. Of the thousands of voiceover actors (beginners and experienced) that I have worked with, they all have the same thing in common; they are active in their career every single day. The ones who are full-time in VO dedicate 6 to 10 hours daily towards marketing, relationship building and auditioning. Those who are part-time put in 2-3 hours a day towards the same. Thriving voiceover actors recognize that they are business owners who just so happen to also be actors. They never lose sight of what it means to be an entrepreneur and master of their own destiny.

Setting Realistic Goals

Your voiceover journey is only beginning. Thank you for purchasing this book and taking steps to educate yourself on this amazing industry.

Now that you have completed this book here are some logical next steps:

1. Read this book again & make full use of all its performance lessons and vocal exercises.

2. Read this book a 3rd time to begin putting its business & marketing information to work. You may also want to purchase the authors book titled <u>How to Set-up and Maintain A BETTER Voiceover Business.</u> It expands upon the business aspects of voiceover.

3. Read other voiceover book titles by the following authors, James Alburger, Elaine Clark, Terry Apple, Joan Baker, Harlan Hogan, & Pat Fraley.

4. Begin seeking out a reputable voiceover coach who can begin to work with you and take your skills to the next level. You may find someone locally or you may need to travel to the ideal coach for you.

5. Begin the process of researching & creating a demo.

6. Set up a business plan & a 1–5 year goal plan.

7. Take your time. Please do not try to rush into this business, slow and steady makes for a well prepared, educated, professional voiceover talent.

8. Use the next page to start setting some basic goals.

1. I will have completed all exercises in this book by _____

2. I will research, select & begin working with a coach by_____

3. I will decide upon my niche or signature sound by_____

4. I will have a quality studio in my home by_____

5. I will have a completed voice over demo by _____

6. I will have a completed website by_____

7. I will have a completed business marketing plan by _____

8. I will make _____# of voice over related calls each week.

9. I will send out & follow up on _____demos each week.

10. I will have 250 'copies' of my demo in circulation by _____

11. I aspire to earn $_____from voiceovers in the next year.

12. I aspire to increase that amount by $_____each year after.

13. I will invest _____% of my voiceover earning back into my business yearly.

14. I will have at least one casting company, talent agent or voiceover marketing company represent me by _____.

15. I will research and attend my first voiceover event or conference in _____(year).

16. I will be a full time, working voiceover actor by_____.

About The Author

Gabrielle Nistico is a voiceover actress with a rewarding career performing national and regional voiceovers for commercial, narration, radio imaging and TV promo clients across the globe.

Her career started in radio as a teenage and since then she has added copywriter, audio producer, casting director, author, voiceover coach, demo and website creator and actress to her resume.

Learn more about Gabby at:
GabrielleNistico.com and VoiceoverVixen.com

VoiceHunter.com is a leading online voiceover casting company. We provide our clients with VO from a select group of highly skilled, reputable voiceover artists. Our casting process is personal & intimate with each client having their own, dedicated casting representative. Gabby has been our operations director since 2003.

VOPrep.com is the newest collaboration between Gabby and the owners of VoiceHunter.com. It brings Gabby's honest, no B.S. approach to the voiceover industry to beginners all across the country. With off-site training options beginners can obtain a quality voiceover education that will give them a solid career foundation.

Practice Scripts - Commercial Copy

SEARS - :15

Hurry into Sears Brand Central for American's biggest appliance & electronics sale – it's going on now. With great low credit options & nationwide service, it's no wonder more people buy top name brands, from the store they trust...Sears.

LYSOL - :15

If you're using a sponge & an ordinary cleaner you might as well be doing this. Fact...Lysol antibacterial kitchen cleaner kills 99.9% of germs that thrive on kitchen surfaces. For cleaning tough grease, no other leading brand is better. Life demands Lysol. That's a fact.

GERBER - :30 Your baby is the reason our standards are so high. At Gerber over 230 research & quality control specialists work to make sure our foods satisfy your baby's taste & nutritional needs. It's your assurance of quality with every Gerber's baby-food product you buy. At Gerber babies are our business & have been for over 50 years.

DESIGN A SIGN: - :30 Commercial Copy

Sometimes all life takes is a great sign. Not like "Hey baby, what's your sign?", an actual sign. Like the plumber's truck that proudly displays "We'll repair what your husband fixed" or the banner at the muffler shop that reads, "No appointment necessary. We hear you coming." so what should your sign say...? Not sure...at Design A Sign, we'll help you figure it out.

BANK OF AMERICA - :30

Home likes simple. Home likes on and off. Hot and cold. Open and closed. Home doesn't care for complicated. Like mortgages that require a degree in economics. That's why we created our Clarify Commitment – a simple, one-page loan summary written in plain language. So whether you're buying a new home, or refinancing your current one, you understand what you're getting. Starting now, home has a new address. Bank of America Home Loans.

STATEFARM - :60

Dear 4,000,000 pounds – You're gone. Goodbye and good riddance! Will you be missed? Hardly. All the pounds we set out to lose will be gone in no time. You wait and see. We worked long and hard over the past two years to kick you to the curb, so don't even think about making a comeback. You used to slow us down. You used to hold us back. NO MORE. Now we've got discipline, commitment, and support on our side. And, as we make progress, our dedication grows stronger. Stronger than YOU. Stronger than ever. You may be lonely right now but don't worry. Pretty soon we hit the 5,000,000 and 10,000,000 marks, you'll have company. Plenty of it. Just remember, as we shed pounds, we gain momentum. It's been real. Liberated and never more dedicated. 50millionpounds.com. Join The Challenge and get all the free tips, tolls, and support you need. Powered by StateFarm.

NIKE LUNARGLIDE - :15 Commercial Copy

Actually, it is rocket science. Nike Lunar-glide. Every foot needs something different. And what they need can change from left foot to right, and from mile one to mile ten. So we took everything we've learned from 36 years of running and delivered a dynamic support innovation that can adjust to every foot out there. Cushion, stability, and Nike without compromises.

Amgen - :30 TV Script

You know how people say, "You're only human?" Well, at Amgen, we believe that deep down some of the very things that make us human like biology & genetics, can be used to create vital medicines to fight serious illness & dramatically improve people's lives. The people at Amgen are using technology to push the limits...of what's humanly possible. Amgen. Proud sponsor of the Amgen Tour of California.

WEIGHT WATCHERS HUNGRY - :60

When you're on a diet, Hungry is in your face all day long.

But with Weight Watchers Online, which you do entirely online, you have what you need to outsmart him, right at your fingertips. Interactive, customizable tools give you structure to make healthier, more satisfying choices. While restaurant guides, 1800 recipes, 31,000 food options, and mobile access give you freedom and flexibility, so you can live life and still lose weight. So no matter how often Hungry shows up, you're in control, and Hungry's, out in the cold. Try it for a week free. Go to weightwathers.com/free and start today. Weight Watchers Online. Stop dieting. Start living.

LITTLE VOICE - :60

Hi, I'm that little voice in your head. You know, the one that pops up every so often to tell you the time is now. I know, I know. You have a lot going on. Family, work. It's been years since you've been in a classroom. I've heard all of the excuses. But you see…I know you and I know this is something you've always dreamed of -going back and getting your MBA…AND from Notre Dame. Their values-based curriculum will give you the skills you need to be a well-rounded leader and ready to take on all the opportunities that come your way. So listen to me. I've never let you down before. The time is now. The Notre Dame Executive MBA program invites you to attend an information reception in South Bend. Which has just been ranked ninth internationally for fastest return on investment by the Wall Street Journal. Attend classes while you work once a month for 21 months: RSVP at executive.nd.edu or call 1-800-631-EMBA.

ATS CORPORATION: - :30

Steven Black from Omaha writes: "On the same day I sent flowers to my friend who was moving to Florida for a job promotion, I also sent flowers to a friend's dad's funeral. To my horror, I later found out that the flower shop got the cards mixed up. The card to the girl moving said 'deepest condolences', the card to the funeral home…'I know it's hot where you're going, but you deserve it.' Needless to say, I have a new florist." Rest assured that at ATS we can tell the difference between funerals & Florida.

QUIT SMOKING CAMPAIGN - :60 Commercial Copy

This needs to sound like a real guy / girl who gets pissed off at anything because he / she just quit smoking.

QUITTER: I said I wanted mustard. Did you not hear me say mustard? I bet this guy heard me say mustard. *You* heard me say mustard, right? Everybody else hear mustard?

QUITTER: Gee Honey. I can't think of anything I'd rather do than pick up deodorant on the way home. Thanks for sprinkling sunshine all over my day.

QUITTER: Why does the hot water take forever to get hot?

QUITTER: Oh. You know what else I hate about puppies?

QUITTER: Have a nice day? What the (BEEP) is that supposed to mean? A "nice" day? Is that sarcasm? Am I a clown to you?

QUITTER: You are without a doubt the stupidest shoe I have ever worn!

ANNCR: Mood swing are just part of quitting smoking. To see the rest. watch Bob kick the habit, and maybe everything else, at bobquits.com.

ANNCR: Mood swing are just part of quitting smoking. To see the rest. watch Jill kick the habit, and maybe everything else, at jillquits.com.

Narration Copy

ARAWAK TRIBE:

Poverty is the closest ally to infectious disease. Poverty prevents education, restricts healthcare & limits human potential. It prevents life for millions of people around the world. It is no coincidence that the world's poorest countries have the highest infectious disease rates on the planet. Quality healthcare & drugs are the most effective means of treatment, & education is necessary to sustain these treatments. These are not luxuries. These are basic human rights.

The Arawak Indians lived on a tiny island in the Caribbean, which they fondly called Haiti. In their native language it means "land of the mountains". In 1492, the Arawaks warmly greeted a fleet of Spanish ships. What greeted them was a regiment of forceful settlers led by Christopher Columbus. The Spaniards went on to abuse these natives to the point of near extinction

Haight-Ashbury – Narration Copy

San Francisco is a city forged by struggle and resistance. From its gold rush beginnings through its earthquake rebirth, the city and its people walk to a different beat to that of the national stride. In the last half of the twentieth century, San Francisco was a sustaining creative environment of concurring generations for counter-culture expression. This environment was nurtured by the collective of people who called San Francisco home. As in any great city, community fuels a movement. San Francisco's Haight-Ashbury is a prime example. Taking cues from the Beats who shaped their own generation a short ten years earlier, The Haight asserted itself as the musical center of the Psychedelic Era.

The Summer of Love was a spontaneous social experiment that melded social conviction and musical expression. Haight-Ashbury was ground zero. Civil rights, the war in Vietnam, sexual liberation and drug experimentation saw a converging flashpoint in this one neighborhood.

Does an activist neighborhood influence a creative process or is it the musical force that informs the social conscience of a community? The Haight will explore this and other questions and our story will be told by those who lived it. With over thirty interviews from members of Jefferson Airplane, Moby Grape, the Grateful Dead as well as the cast of characters who lived in the Haight, we see how a neighborhood and its musical soul changed America.

Rock n' roll photojournalist Don Aters captured images of all the major players of the time. Aters has given us complete access to his full collection of photos from the Haight. He takes us on a tour through the Haight, showing us the Haight-Ashbury of yesterday and the search for the unbroken thread that ties it to today.

And what of the Haight of today? Are the ideals that define this neighborhood still a living, breathing force or is it now a wistful movement of residual nostalgia. When we walk the streets of the neighborhood today do we still see a vibrant center of resistance or more accurately, a tourist destination. The Haight is a timeless tale of making a difference. The demographic for this program is wide. It's appeal spans the over 76 million Baby Boomers who lived through these times as well as the generations that followed and still live the dream.

Robert Howell Brooks – Narration Copy
The reign of our world-wide wing commander, Robert Howell Brooks has ended. Known as Howell to his family, RH, Bob or Mr. B to the world, his life positively impacted thousands along his path. Robert H. Brooks --successful entrepreneur, philanthropist, sports enthusiast are just a few of the words used to describe the man. His mother and father barely scratched an existence from the South

Carolina soil while raising six children. This rigorous childhood prepared him for the tough battleground of the business world. He pushed himself hard as if he knew his time would not be terribly long and he had much to accomplish. He lived with severe diabetes for more than half his 70 years and hoped through his support a cure would be found in his lifetime. Brook's upbringing made him tough and driven, and he drove those around him to accomplish more than they ever imagined they could. Over and over Bob heard his detractors say it "can't be done" only to prove them wrong. With a food science degree from Clemson university in hand Brooks pioneered a process for non-dairy vegetable creamers that enabled him to start Eastern Foods, a food distribution company that has serviced every major domestic and International airline along with countless major restaurant and grocery chains throughout America. A prodigious businessman never satisfied to sit still long, he launched the successful national retail brand Naturally Fresh, the first all natural, preservative free salad dressings, sauces and dips. He parlayed those proceeds into ownership of the trademark of Hooters Restaurants, one of the most recognizable brands in the world today. His company Hooters of America is the single largest owner and operator of Hooters Restaurants. Hooters sponsorship of Alan Kulwicki lead them to a Winston cup trophy after one complete season in the sport. Brooks recently ventured into the troubled airline industry convinced his no nonsense business style could transform a stodgy industry. Experts predicted it would be three years before Hooters Air could launch, but in reality, he bought, painted and launched a fleet of planes under the Hooters Airline banner in less than six months. A prolific philanthropist his motto and creed "to whom much is given much is expected" was followed throughout his life. Through his Hooters Community Endowment fund, Brooks has generously given away more than 8 million dollars. His accomplishments, far and wide, led some to say his was a storied and lucky life. But tragedy was not a stranger. A corporate plane crash in 1993 stole the life of his 26 year old son Mark along with the lives of three of his closest friends including champion Alan Kulwicki and forever changing Brooks. Intent on turning bad into good, Brooks used the loss to start the USAR Pro Cup series in honor of those lost. It's a place where young racers come to hone their skills and it endures today to keep alive the legacy of Alan and the others lost on that terrible day. We now say goodbye to a man who drove himself to wealth and greatness; who persevered through tragedy and a man who realized late in life his greatest assets were his children. His was a life well-lived --and oh how he lived----He lived passionately. Not bad for a man just winging it!

THE MAGIC BOX - Narration Copy

Here's a story that might be hard to believe. But there are those who say this really, truly happened. One bright, sunshiny day, a little girl & her brother were walking down a very busy street, in a very busy way. The girl's name was Julia, and her brother's name was Jason. The two children were walking—and talking—when suddenly, Jason stopped—bent down—& picked up a little box. The box looked very special. It was grey….and had a fuzzy, curved top. Jason opened the box to find a sparkling, blue & green ring. Carved into the round face of the ring was a little picture of our globe—the kind of picture astronauts see when they look down at earth from way up high in space. Suddenly, a small piece of paper fluttered out of the box…onto the sidewalk. It landed right at his sister's feet. So Julia bent down, picked up the note, & read it out loud. It said…

Cleveland County Healthcare System – Narration Copy

Cleveland County Healthcare System provides the area with premier service, quality, and care. Representing two hospitals, two extended care facilities, home health, hospice, and a network of physicians, it plays an integral role in maintaining the health and well being of each person in the county. Established Centers of Excellence provide a centralized approach to care that exists throughout the entire system.

A unique partnership with Carolinas HealthCare System, in addition to local governance, allows physicians and their patients access to specialized services within one of the largest networks in the nation. Our acute care facilities employ more than 1500 people who serve 241 beds at Cleveland Regional Medical Center and 102 beds at Kings Mountain Hospital. Specialized Centers such as Blumenthal Cancer, Cardiovascular, Diabetes, Pain, and Women's Life add to the wealth of options provided for our patients. Designated as the first level III trauma center in North Carolina, Cleveland Regional offers comprehensive care, advanced resources, and a highly skilled medical staff. Helicopter transport services are available for patients requiring tertiary specialties.

At Kings Mountain Hospital there is a commitment to offer multiple community-based specialized services. The latest in diagnostic radiology coupled with top-notch programs in Behavioral Health, Physical Therapy and Outpatient Clinics support the hospital's mission in providing personalized treatment. Within Cleveland County Healthcare System, more than 300 Physicians share their talents to be the healthcare provider of choice for Cleveland County and the surrounding areas. Our commitment to those we serve extends beyond saving lives.

We also focus on sustaining lives through ongoing educational activities, programs and events that raise awareness. This mindset is carried throughout the entire health care system and keeps the bond with the community strong. The family approach to working and living is what has made Cleveland County the place of comfort and growth. Residents can enjoy the laid back and quiet approach to living in a small town thanks to the areas quaint and charming shops. Or, they can join in the hustle and bustle of a larger city at events like free summer concert series.

THE COLUMBIA INFERNO – Narration Copy

IN 1999, THE COLLEGE TOWN OF COLUMBIA SC LEARNED THAT IT WOULD SOON HAVE A NEW TEAM AND A NEW SPORT TO PULL FOR.

SINCE THEN, THE WORLDS OF SOUTHERN CULTURE AND PROFESSIONAL ICE HOCKEY HAVE EMERGED TO FORM A STRONG COMPETITIVE TEAM, A DEDICATED STAFF, AND A LOYAL FAN FOLLOWING.

THE COLUMBIA INFERNO FIND THEMSELVES PLAYING IN THE SHADOWS OF A BUILDING THAT HOSTS A SOUTH CAROLINA BASKETBALL DYNASTY AS THEY ENTER THEIR SEVENTH SEASON IN THE FRANK MCGUIRE ARENA.

NOW IN THE FINAL PLANNING STAGES OF THEIR OWN ARENA, THE COLUMBIA INFERNO IS EAGER TO SHOW YOU, THEIR FANS, THAT THEY ARE HERE TO STAY.

IN A LEAGUE WITH LOTS OF RIVALS, COACH TROY MANN WILL PULL THIS TEAM OF NEW PLAYERS AND SEASONED VETERANS TOGETHER TO SKATE HARD AND WIN BIG!

IT'S A LONG AND TOUGH SCHEDULE AS COLUMBIA'S INFERNO ENTER THEIR SEVENTH SEASON. COULD HARD WORK AND SKILLED PLAYERS MAKE THIS LUCKY NUMBER 7 FOR OUR INFERNO?

GET READY AS WE FOLLOW SEVERAL OF YOUR COLUMBIA INFERNO PLAYERS AS THEY FIND OUT WHAT IT TAKES TO PLAY FOR THE KELLY CUP. WILL THEY GET BURNED, OR WILL THEY SQUELCH THE COMPETITION AND ACHIEVE THE TITLE OF ECHL CHAMPIONS?

Snap Genie – Phone Prompt

1. SnapGenie, your voice, your photos, your story…

2. Myfamily.com IS excited to offer you this beta version of a new feature called SnapGenie.

3. SnapGenie makes it easier than ever to share your photos in a fun, Interesting, intimate, and engaging way. In a matter of minutes, you can easily bundle narrated photo slide shows just like the one you are watching.

4. All it takes is a computer connected to the Internet and a telephone or cell phone.

5. To get started, simply go to www.snapgenie.com and create an account. If you already have a MyFamily account you can use your own login information

6. Next select the photos you want to use and upload them. When your photos are uploaded, you'll be directed to the telephone studio where 'vve'll provide you ilvith a phone number you'll use to cal! and narrate your slide show. Once you're done, all you have to do is save it then share it with friends and family! It's easy and fun for everyone.

7. Do you know someone who would like to see this SnapGenie show? Just click the "share this" button below and enter the email addresses of the person you'd like us to pass it along to, or start sharing your own pictures and stories with friends and family today. It's easy and free.

8. Myfamily.com is excited to bring you SnapGenie. In a matter of minutes you can easily build narrated photo slide shows just like the one you are watching. All it takes is a computer connected to the Internet and a telephone or cell phone.

HAMPTON INN - MESSAGE ON HOLD COPY

How do you like your breakfast? We hope hot & fresh. Come taste our hot breakfast—from 6 to 9 every morning. We call it our "on the house" breakfast & hot's our new thing…hot eggs, hot sausage & hot biscuits…very tasty starts. Add a fresh cup of our premium blend coffee, a selection of fresh fruit & suddenly, you're starting off with a smile.

When you stay at Hampton, we want you to be 100% satisfied. That's why we promise friendly service, clean rooms, & comfortable surroundings every time, every stay. If you're not satisfied, we don't expect you to pay. That's our personal guarantee to you…

The weekend's coming up. Got any big plans? How about doing something fun with your kids, or maybe getting away with your somebody special…take a trip…go some place new…be together? At Hampton Inn weekends dot com, we have lots of great getaway ideas. From sporting events & outdoor attractions to local festivals & cool outings. Fun weekend ideas are right at your fingertips at Hampton Inn weekends dot com.

Smart Business Credit – Message on Hold Copy

Thank you again for calling Smart Business Credit -Equipment Financing Solutions for your business. We appreciate your call and your patience -we'll be with you in just a moment. Smart Business Credit started with one purpose in mind; to provide an avenue for small to medium sized businesses to obtain the much needed, and sometimes difficult to acquire, financing for equipment purchases vital to their growth and development. Since then, we have built strong relationships across the country based on trust and integrity. Unlike other organizations, Smart Business Credit offers a variety of financing solutions for your business. Our expert Lenders will meet with you and discuss your specific needs. We'll then go to work, searching for the program that is best suited for your business needs. Ready to get started? Just visit w-w-w dot smart business credit dot com and click on "apply now". We'll return to the line in just a moment to assist you. Whether you are a new company, just starting out, or a long established business, Smart Business Credit will provide you with the expertise to obtain the equipment you need today. With our latest technology you are only minutes away from being approved. Ask us more when we return to the line. If you are a dealer, ask us about our Smart Partner programs. We know that our clients have special and unique needs. As a result, we offer a wide variety of plans and services to fit those needs. For more information visit us online at w-w-w dot smart business credit dot com.

Industrial Scripts

PropertyTract -

PropertyTract, a division of TractManager, is a technology-based contract and document management service provider serving the Real Estate industry.

The company's solutions help real estate professionals regain control of their operating contracts and lease documents used in the management of their real estate portfolios. PropertyTract provides intelligent control of your contracts by allowing you to:

Track terms of real estate leases

Track terms of building maintenance contracts

Store and distribute asset management reports

Create a Due Diligence database

Create custom reports of contract information and costs

PropertyTract's contract management solution provides real estate companies with on-line, real time access to a customized database of their lease and operating contract information. This presentation will demonstrate some of the uses and applications in a real estate operation. To log onto the database, a User goes to the PropertyTract website, selects the Secure Login button, enters a User Name and Password and clicks OK. (Short Pause) Various levels of user access and permissions are available within each database.

PropertyTract is broken up into three separate databases: Service Contracts, Leasing, and Closing books. Let's first take a look at the Service Contracts.

The database is customized to your organization by Region, Portfolio/Owner, Building, Contract Types, and Vendor. The database is currently being viewed by building. By selecting "view all" a user can identify all service contract files within each building. This view will show all of the contract files that each building has.

The user will immediately be able to identify the contract type, vendor, and expiration of each agreement, along with a link to each contract relationship file.

By clicking on the link the user can view the Contract Relationship File. Our personnel create a contract cover sheet for the relationship file, for each scanned contract. Each contract cover sheet lists critical information concerning the contract. Here we can see that City Cooling Inc. has been contracted by ABC Funds, for HVAC Services for the identified Buildings and portfolio. The agreement expires May 31, 2009 and the estimated monthly charge is $15,000 or $0.15 per square foot. Mike Turner, as the Building Manager is the primary party responsible for this contract file.

AMERICAN AIRLINES - Industrial

Welcome aboard American Airlines coast-to-coast service. We'll be happy to do everything possible to make your flight with us a most pleasurable experience. We'll provide you with all the information you need to know about your flight, your destination, and the equipment on which you are currently flying. In addition, we are proud to present our American Airlines feature film presentation, for our transcontinental passengers. We'd like you now to remove the plastic insert found directly in front of you in the seat back pocket. Please review the safety information during the flight for your own protection, in the unlikely event of an in-flight emergency.

FACA Pitch - Industrial

NARRATOR Ladies and Gentlemen: Live from Las Vegas, the American Concert Awards with your host...

Today, artists stake their careers and their fortunes on creating unforgettable live concert performances. Today, staggering numbers of fans are going to their concerts.

$3.1 billion in concert tickets was spent in 2005. The top 100 tours sold a total of 36.3 million tickets. Internet bidding wars for hot tickets are exploding. And all these numbers continue to skyrocket.

Long overdue, Timeless Communications presents the American Concert Awards - hip, sexy, and relevant, it's an awards show that will dominate all others.

The fans have their favorite concert. They will want to see how their favorite concert rates against others. And since the artists will be showing off their performance skills, not just their music, this will be must see TV.

Advertisers aligning themselves with today's mind-blowing tours will want to be a part of the American Concert Awards. Tour sponsors will jockey with each other to create Superbowl-level ads.
Produced by Timeless Communications, the industry leader of live events, the judges will be made up of print, radio, and TV music media personalities from major markets.

This not only maintains the integrity of the awards, but also creates valuable cross-promotion. The final award of the evening, the Concert of the Year Award, will be voted on by the television audience, who can text message their vote. Exciting Visually overwhelming. Immensely entertaining television. Not your father's award show ... The American Concert Awards.

Ernst & Young - Industrial

"Welcome to EmTech 08 [pronounced as one word -M-tech oh-eight]. Technology Review's 8th annual Emerging Technologies Conference at MIT [em-eye-tee]. Each year EmTech brings together world-class innovators and technology leaders, to demonstrate and discuss the most important technologies that will have a dramatic impact on our world. "

"Today the spotlight is on Women in Technology. Afti Riazi [AH-tee ree-AH-zee] from Ogilvy and Mather, Lisa Su from Freescale, and other experts will expand your knowledge about networking in the real world, developing leadership, and fostering innovation. We'll close the day with an MIT

Enterprise Forum *global broadcast that will explore the different pathways to entrepreneurship taken by some leading women innovators. "*

Part 2 Wednesday

"Today you'll learn how Vinod Khosla [Vin-OHD KOHS-Ia] plans to invent the future with renewable energy, hear expert panels discuss what's next for green transportation and mobile technologies, and socialize with Gina Bianchini [GEE-na BEE-ahn-KEY-nee] of Ning. We'll discuss the future of Cloud Computing and the Web, hear about how engineers are connecting chips with light, and meet this year's TR35 [pronounce individual letters then the number thirty five-not, three five], the top innovators under the age of 35.

Part 3 Thursday

"Today you'll experience how Microsoft's Craig Mundie [MUN-dee] sees the future of computing, have a fireside chat with Desh Desponde [desh des-PAHN-day], document Sophie Vandebroek's [VAN-de-brooks] perspective on Xerox, and ponder how technology is influencing the way we vote.

We'll hear about how parallel computing is becoming mainstream, genomics is starting to get personal, and the open-source ethos is influencing hardware design. And we'll come together one last time to listen to an innovative performance by Zoe *Keating [ZOH-ee}.*

Foot and Ankle Wellness Center: Voiceover Text - Industrial

Dr. leonard Vekkos started practicing podiatry well over twenty years ago. Board Certified in Foot and Ankle Surgery and a Fellow with the American College of Primary Podiatric Medicine and Orthopedics, Dr. Vekkos had a dream of what effective podiatric care could be. The doctor envisioned bringing together a group of healthcare professionals under one roof who were dedicated to providing patients with state-of-the-art facilities, physicians with advanced training and a staff committed to the highest quality patient care. In 2003, this dream became a reality with the formation of the Foot and Ankle Wellness Center at Seven Bridges.

In just a short time the Foot and Ankle Wellness Center has realized explosive growth, validation of the need for this type of "outside the box" approach to podiatric healthcare. The Center strives to address all of a patient's needs in a single location with a staff of professionals dedicated to a patient's health and well-being. The Center offers the latest in cutting edge services: on-site X-Ray Services advanced Digital Radiology, on-site Diagnostic Ultrasound, on-site Physical Therapy for rehabilitation, an on-site Pedicure Spa and an on-site, state-of-the art, accredited surgical facility.

The vision of the Foot and Ankle Wellness Center is one of trust and compassion. It's a practice that strives to listen to a patient's concerns while taking the time to answer any of their questions. Those who come through the Center's doors are more than patients. They're our friends, our neighbors, our community.

Probably the best example of the Center's alternative approach to foot healthcare is the Wellness for the Sole. Especially-built room offers a secluded and calming atmosphere for pedicures and foot and ankle massages in a private, personal and relaxing environment.
A medical facility can be a frightening place *for* a young child. The Foot and Ankle Wellness Center takes great pride 'in its extensive experience and expertise in children's care. The Center consciously avoids the sterile, intimidating surroundings of so many other medical offices. You won't see any lab coats at the Foot and Ankle Wellness Center. What you will see is a professional decorum in a calming environment. An atmosphere that is welcoming to the entire family.

The Foot and Ankle Wellness Center is a constantly growing healthcare facility, built to evolve in an ever-changing medical field. While the Center dedicates itself to offer the latest technological advances and techniques, there are some things that will always remain constant -and that's a staff that takes pride in the relationships they build with patients, healthcare professionals and the community at large.

RADIO IMAGING COPY

- The classic rock station – only the best on New York's only classic rock station – WRCN.

- This is where the rock lives – & drinks all of our beer – rocking you with 40 minute nonstop rock blocks every hour of everyday – 94 WYSP – the rock of Philadelphia.

- Garth Brooks, Shania Twain, Clint Black & all your favorites come alive, everyday on Jacksonville's number one station for hit country – Cat country – 103.5, WXRZ.

- Detroit's home for blazin' hits & R&B – this is Hot 98.1

- We've got all the jamz you love from the 70's, 80's, 90's & today. Ya dig? Let it flow with KBRT.

- Smooth tracks for a smooth town – KZ 101 – we're playing all your smooth jazz favorites all day & all night.

- Music the whole family can listen to. You won't find offensive music or disc jockeys here. Just great wholesome music you can enjoy anytime. We are WJHC

- Turn off the noise & tune into the light – K-Lite your choice for contemporary christian hits.

- Get all the news, talk & sports you need everyday. We're your information station – K-F-A-N, Phoenix, Scottsdale, Mesa – 105.9 The Fan.

- Bone crunching sports, hard hitting news & informative talk – & we call it work. You'll call it great radio – 105.9 The Fan.

TV PROMO COPY

- A story of courage. A story of hope. A story of the love between mother & daughter. A true story that has touched the hearts of millions. Lifetime presents Oscar winner Sally Field in Not Without My Daughter. Sunday night at 9 only on Lifetime.

- Saturday at 11. Most people are turning to these supplements to ease their pain. But new tests say some are missing a key ingredient...Which one really gives you a jump on joint pain relief? Find out on Eyewitness News.

- It seems like everyone is pitching a low carb diet. But don't believe all the hype. NBC 3 puts some of today's most popular low carbohydrate foods to the test. We'll cut through the come-ons & give you the true "lowdown on low carbs". Thursday on NBC news at 6.

- Rubies, Diamonds, Gold...find out what Riches await you on an all new episode of Cash & Treasures; tonight at 9 on the Travel Channel.

- Laughs on Late is too funny to miss. We're got all your Friends, Scrubs, & Two & a Half men. This is seriously funny television. Laughs on Late, every weekday at 11 on MY Q2.

- Tomorrow on The Office, Jim has to defend his coffee mug while Pam becomes an eavesdropper. Meanwhile, Andy is anxiously trying to secure details about his and Angela's wedding, but Angela isn't as willing. Don't miss an all new The Office tomorrow night at 9 on NBC Channel 36.

- Tonight on Family Guy…After Peter's dad dies, he finds out that his real father lives in Ireland; Stewie realizes that he likes when Lois spanks him, so he purposely gets into trouble. TBS tonight at 8.

- While searching for stolen cargo, john becomes separated from the group. Agent Ellison's murder investigation leads him to a surprising suspect. Can john prove himself to be a great military leader capable of stopping Sky Net? Terminator: the Sarah Conner chronicles, Monday at 8 on fox.

- You know that feeling when you realize that you're dreaming? You're not awake but you know it's a dream. That is how his whole life has felt because nothing has ever felt completely real; its all been a very convincing imitation, Dexter's house of horrors. Dexter… the new season premieres September 28 at 9 only on Showtime.

- Swat (special weapons and tactics) moves to new time. Starting Monday, catch the team weeknights at 6 on channel 9.

- Mark your calendars, because this fall it's time for a new… everything every Friday night. Someone has a secret. On the next Degrassi the truth comes out way before it's ready. Don't miss an all new episode tonight at 8 only on N! TV for teens.

- You voted for your favorite actors, artists, and even Indy car drivers. Be sure to watch the results as Miley Cyrus hosts the 2008 Teen Choice Awards where the coolest stars will receive coveted Teen Choice surfboard awards in categories such as Choice Male Hottie and Choice Hook-Up. TEEN CHOICE 2008, Aug. 4th at 8:00 on FOX.

- The year 2035… where robots are programmed to improve the lives of humans…But could the newest model be programmed to kill? Will Smith… Bridget Moynahan… "I Robot".

- Nothing that lives in the imagination is more frightening than the terror that lives in Castlerock Maine. From the novel by Stephen King, creator of Carrie and The Shining, comes a startling vision of fear… Cujo, Friday night at 10 on Sci-Fi.

- The true story of the song that inspired the world and the man who changed history. One man will risk everything to speak for those who could not, to make the blind see, and to lead a movement that would change the world… Amazing Grace on the Inspiration Network Sunday night at 7.

- On the next Entertainment Tonight, Were Jennifer Aniston and John Mayer on a double date with Nicole Richie and Joel Madden? And, An emotional **Angelina Jolie** was moved to tears at a London press conference for her new film 'Changeling' on Monday. But what made her break down? Tonight at 7:30 on WSOC Channel 9.

- Heather, Lindsay, Paris, Nicole – what do all these Hollywood starlets have in common? Find out on Wake-Up Rising tomorrow morning at 7am – right here on Fox Phoenix.

CPSIA information can be obtained
at www.ICGtesting.com
Printed in the USA
BVHW040733090819
555488BV00001B/103/P